Eerie ARKANSAS

Heather Woodward

THE
History
PRESS

Published by The History Press
Charleston, SC
www.historypress.com

Copyright © 2023 by Heather Woodward
All rights reserved
First published 2023

Manufactured in the United States

ISBN 9781467154529

Library of Congress Control Number: 2023938360

Notice: The information in this book is true and complete to the best of our knowledge. It is offered without guarantee on the part of the author or The History Press. The author and The History Press disclaim all liability in connection with the use of this book.

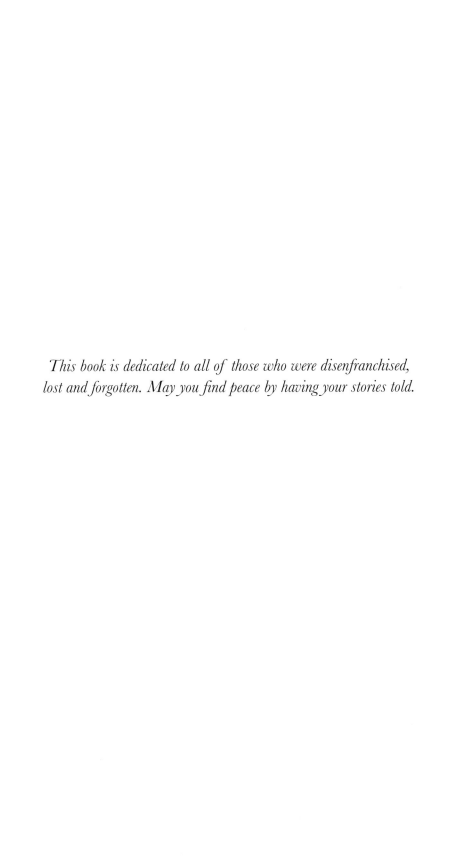

This book is dedicated to all of those who were disenfranchised, lost and forgotten. May you find peace by having your stories told.

CONTENTS

ACKNOWLEDGEMENTS

Kelli Welsh—for stomping through haunted forests and jagged ruins with me. You are the *best* paranormal companion.

Stephanie Carrell—for letting me spiral and for joining me in the game.

Tyler Ross—for existing and making life interesting.

My mom—for getting excited every time I tell you I'm writing another book.

Buck Mulle—for taking pictures and being adventurous.

Cashew—for being my new forest buddy.

Michael—for telling me all kinds of stories and taking me to all kinds of crazy places.

INTRODUCTION

UNVEILING THE HAUNTING LEGENDS AND DARK HISTORY OF THE NATURAL STATE

Arkansas is a state known for its breathtaking woods, crystal deposits and diverse history. However, what many people do not know is that beneath the tranquil exterior of this state lies a world of supernatural strangeness, haunted locations and chilling legends. This is a book that takes you on a journey through some of the most haunted places in Arkansas, exploring the stories behind them and delving into the strange and unexplainable occurrences that continue to take place. I went to investigate many of the places in the book with my friend Kelli. We have documented our findings to let you know if the legend and lore meet up with reality.

One of the most famous and eerie legends in Arkansas is that of the Gurdon Light, located near Gurdon in Clark County. Witnesses have reported seeing a mysterious light moving across the railroad tracks, disappearing and reappearing at random intervals.

Another eerie light phenomenon in Arkansas is the Dover Light, located near the town of Dover in Pope County. Described as a glowing orb or light that moves through the woods, the Dover Light continues to intrigue and mystify visitors.

In addition to light phenomena, Arkansas is known for its poltergeist activity. The Mena Poltergeist is one of the most famous cases of poltergeist activity in the state. Witnesses have reported seeing objects moving by themselves, hearing strange noises and even experiencing physical attacks by an unseen force.

Aside from poltergeists, Arkansas is also home to many haunted locations. One of the most well-known is the Crescent Hotel in Eureka Springs. Guests and staff alike have reported hearing strange noises, seeing ghostly apparitions and even having encounters with the spirits of past guests.

In addition to haunted locations, Arkansas is known for its sightings of cryptids. One of the most famous is the Boggy Creek Monster, also known as the Fouke Monster. This creature is said to inhabit the swamps and forests of southern Arkansas.

The Natural State is also the home of the infamous case of the West Memphis Three, which gained national attention in the early 1990s. Three teenagers were accused and convicted of the brutal murders of three young boys in West Memphis, Arkansas. The case was highly controversial, with many believing the teenagers were wrongfully convicted because of the Satanic Panic, which is still plaguing the culture today.

In this book, we take a deep dive into these and other eerie and supernatural happenings in Arkansas. We explore the legends and lore that continue to fascinate and terrify visitors and examine the possible explanations behind the unexplainable. From the mysterious lights to haunted locations and cryptids, Arkansas is a state full of surprises and secrets waiting to be uncovered. Join me on this journey through the dark and eerie side of Arkansas as we uncover the haunting legends and dark history that continue to make this state a place of mystery and intrigue.

A Brief History of the Natural State

Arkansas has a rich and intricate history spanning thousands of years, as many Native tribes, including the Caddo, Quapaw and Osage, have inhabited the land. These tribes developed unique cultures and ways of life that continue to influence the state today.

The Spanish were the first Europeans to explore Arkansas in the sixteenth century, but it wasn't until the seventeenth century that European settlements were established in the area. The French established a trading post at Arkansas Post in 1686, which became a hub for trade with Natives. The French ruled over Arkansas for much of the eighteenth century until they ceded control of the territory to Spain in 1763. Arkansas was returned to France in 1800 as part of the Treaty of San Ildefonso and later became part of the United States through the Louisiana Purchase in 1803.

During the nineteenth century, Arkansas was primarily an agricultural state, with cotton as its main crop. The state was divided over the issue of slavery and seceded from the Union to join the Confederacy during the Civil War. The state was the site of several major Civil War battles, including the Battle of Pea Ridge and the Battle of Prairie Grove.

After the Civil War, Arkansas faced significant challenges as it struggled to rebuild its economy and society. The state was occupied by Union forces for several years, and the process of Reconstruction was fraught with tension and conflict. However, by the turn of the twentieth century, Arkansas was experiencing significant growth and development. In the early twentieth century, the state was known for its timber and mineral resources, and it became a major center of the oil and gas industry in the 1920s.

Arkansas played a significant role in the civil rights movement, with the Little Rock Nine incident in 1957 drawing national attention. Today, the state has a diverse economy and is known for its natural beauty, with the Ozark and Ouachita Mountains offering stunning vistas and outdoor recreation opportunities. The state is also home to several important cultural institutions, including the Crystal Bridges Museum of American Art and the Clinton Presidential Library.

Slavery in Arkansas

Arkansas was a slave state before the Civil War, and the practice of slavery was deeply entrenched in the state's economy and society. By 1860, there were around 111,000 slaves in Arkansas, making up about 25 percent of the state's population.

The politics of the time were dominated by the issue of slavery and states' rights. Many white politicians in Arkansas were proslavery, and they strongly opposed any efforts to restrict or abolish the practice. In fact, Arkansas was one of the last states to secede from the Union and join the Confederacy, largely due to its commitment to the institution of slavery.

However, not all white Arkansans were proslavery. There were some abolitionists and antislavery activists in the state, although they were in the minority. Additionally, some white Arkansans opposed slavery not because they believed it was morally wrong but because they believed it hurt the economic interests of poor white farmers.

The enslaved in Arkansas faced many hardships and abuses. They were forced to work long hours in brutal conditions, and they had few legal rights or protections. Many of the enslaved people in Arkansas were separated from their families, as they were bought and sold by slave traders.

THE CIVIL WAR IN ARKANSAS

The Civil War in Arkansas began in May 1861, when the state seceded from the Union and joined the Confederacy. The decision to secede was not a unanimous one, and there was significant opposition from Unionists in the state. Nevertheless, Governor Henry Rector and the state legislature voted to secede, and Arkansas became the ninth state to join the Confederacy.

In the early years of the war, Arkansas was relatively quiet, as most of the fighting took place elsewhere in the Confederacy. However, that changed in 1862, when Union forces launched a series of campaigns to gain control of the Mississippi River. Arkansas, which lay along the western bank of the river, became a key battleground.

The first major battle in Arkansas was the Battle of Pea Ridge, which was fought on March 7–8, 1862, in Benton County. Union forces under the command of General Samuel R. Curtis faced off against Confederate forces under the command of General Earl Van Dorn. The battle was fought in difficult terrain with steep hills and dense forests.

The Confederate army, numbering around sixteen thousand, had been marching toward the Union army at Pea Ridge with the intention of engaging them in battle. The Union army, with around ten thousand soldiers, had taken up positions on the ridge with artillery stationed on the high ground.

On the morning of March 7, the Confederate army launched a surprise attack on the Union positions, hoping to catch them off guard. However, the Union army was well-prepared, and the battle quickly turned into a fierce and bloody struggle.

The Confederate army made several attempts to break through the Union lines, but they were repulsed each time. The Union artillery proved to be a decisive factor, with well-placed shots causing significant damage to the Confederate ranks.

The battle raged on throughout the day, with both sides suffering heavy losses. By the end of the day, the Confederate army had been forced to retreat to a nearby town, leaving the Union army in control of the battlefield.

The second day of the battle saw the Union army launch a counterattack, which proved to be successful. The Confederate army was once again forced to retreat, and the Union army pursued them for several miles, inflicting further losses.

Despite being outnumbered, the Union forces were able to stave off the Confederate attack and secure a key victory. The Battle of Pea Ridge was significant because it prevented the Confederates from regaining control of Missouri and secured Union control of northern Arkansas.

Following the Battle of Pea Ridge, Union forces pushed deeper into Arkansas, and in September 1862, they clashed with Confederate forces at the Battle of Prairie Grove in Washington County. The battle was fought on December 7, 1862, and it was one of the largest and bloodiest Civil War battles fought in Arkansas. Union forces, led by General James G. Blunt, faced off against Confederate forces led by General Thomas C. Hindman. The battle was fought in and around the town of Prairie Grove and was characterized by fierce fighting and heavy casualties on both sides. Ultimately, the Union forces were barely able to secure a victory.

The Confederate army, numbering around eleven thousand, had marched into Arkansas with the intention of stopping the Union advance.

The Union army, with around ten thousand soldiers, had taken up positions on the high ground near Prairie Grove, with artillery stationed on the ridges. The Confederate army launched a surprise attack on the Union positions, hoping to catch them off guard.

The battle quickly turned into a fierce and bloody struggle, with both sides suffering heavy losses. The Confederate army made several attempts to break through the Union lines, but they were repulsed each time.

The Union artillery proved to be a decisive factor in the battle, with well-placed shots causing considerable damage to the Confederate ranks. The battle raged on throughout the day, with neither side gaining a clear advantage.

By nightfall, the Confederate army had been forced to retreat, leaving the Union army in control of the battlefield. The Battle of Prairie Grove was a significant victory for the Union army, as it allowed them to continue their advance into Arkansas and establish a strong presence in the state.

After the Battle of Prairie Grove, the Confederate forces retreated southward to regroup and reorganize. The Union army, on the other hand, remained in the area and consolidated its hold on Northwest Arkansas. This victory was a turning point for Union forces in Arkansas and helped solidify their control over the region. In addition, it was a significant morale boost for the Union troops, who had previously experienced defeat and setbacks in the region.

The following year, in March 1863, Union forces, under the command of General Samuel R. Curtis, again clashed with Confederate troops, this time at the Battle of Fayetteville. This battle, also known as the Battle of West Fork, was a smaller engagement than the two earlier battles but was still significant. Union forces under the command of General James Blunt attacked Confederate forces under the command of General William L. Cabell. The Confederates were outnumbered and outgunned, and after a brief engagement, they withdrew from the area.

Following this battle, Union forces in Arkansas continued to secure their hold on the region, but Confederate troops remained active and continued to conduct raids and guerrilla attacks. One such attack occurred in April 1864, when Confederate general Sterling Price led a raid into Missouri from Arkansas. The raid was successful at first, but Union forces under the command of General William T. Sherman pursued and defeated Price's forces in the Battle of Westport in Missouri.

Despite this setback, Confederate troops continued to fight in Arkansas until the end of the war. In May 1865, Confederate general Kirby Smith surrendered his forces, including those in Arkansas, to Union general Edward Canby, effectively ending the Civil War in the state.

The Civil War had a profound impact on Arkansas. The state was devastated by the conflict, with much of its infrastructure destroyed and its economy in ruins. The war also had a lasting impact on the state's political and social landscape. In the aftermath of the war, the state was occupied by Union troops, and a Republican government was established. This government oversaw the process of reconstruction, which aimed to rebuild the state and integrate freed Black people into society.

PART I

LORE AND LEGENDS

GIANTS IN THE OZARKS

BEAVER LAKE

According to the *New Age Magazine* (vol. 18, 1913) article titled "The Whiteriver Trails," written by the well-known and highly trusted reporter Victor Schoffelmeyer, a set of giant skeleton remains were found by an older "hillbilly" in a cave just outside of Eureka Springs, Arkansas. One of the skulls was perfectly intact, and when it was added to the other remains, the skeleton stood nearly ten feet tall.

The following is an excerpt from the original article:

> *While the historical features of the Ozarks held our attention, by far the most fascinating discovery was one made by an aged recluse and naturalist who for ten years had lived in a shelter cave near where we camped. "Dad" Riggins spent much of his time digging in the ashes which form the floor of many of these caves. At a depth of more than three feet he found the remains of several giant human skeletons, including an almost perfect skull which differed in many particulars from a modern specimen. When partly joined the largest skeleton was almost ten feet tall. "Dad" Riggins showed us hieroglyphics covering the Palisades thought to be thousands of years old.*

In the television episode "In Search for the Lost Giants" (*A Photo, a Tooth, the Truth*, season 1, episode 2), the Vieira brothers traveled to Northwest Arkansas to search for the cave mentioned in the article. But they were met with a major drawback. The cave entrance was thirty-five feet underwater due to the building of the Beaver Dam in the early 1960s. The brothers enlisted the help of Mike Young, who had dived all over the world looking for skulls and relics.

Bill Vieira and Young dove into Beaver Lake, searching for the mouth of the cave. They discovered the entrance, along with a set of stacked stones that functioned as a retaining wall. The lake was murky and silty. So, Young took a camera back into the cave to get footage to view at a later date.

Back at their hotel, the Vieira brothers reviewed the footage of the dive. They didn't find anything pertaining to the bones in the article. However, they did speculate there were pictographs of a face and a wolf in the cave.

AIRSHIPS OF ARKANSAS

OUACHITA MOUNTAINS

THE MAN WITH THE SMOKE-COLORED GLASSES

Between 1897 and 1898, there were a series of airship sightings across the Ouachita Mountains. According to an article from the *Arkansas Gazette*, on April 21, 1897, a conductor for the Iron Mountain Railroad visited Texarkana to pick up a part to bring back to his workplace in Little Rock, Arkansas. The engine in question was not ready yet, so while he waited, he decided to go hunting in the woods near Coleman.

He had been hunting for about three hours in the woods when he distinctly heard the sound of an air brake. Curious about the sound, the railroad employee investigated the area. Off in the distance, about a few acres away, he saw what looked like an airship. He had read about the mysterious craft in the newspaper and knew there had been sightings across the country from California to Texas and now, he suspected, in Arkansas.

The hunter crept closer, and aboard the ship, he saw a man with smoke-colored glasses emerge.

He walked up to the glasses-wearing man and asked, "Is this the airship?" The man replied, "Yes, sir."

While the hunter was walking forward and engaging with the spectacle-wearing man, a few more people came out of the airship.

Curious about the craft, the man asked the group on the airship about the sound he had heard. He wondered if it was the sound of an air brake.

The man with smoke-colored glasses said they were using airplane parts and compressed air and that in the future, everyone would learn more about the technology.

THE JESSIEVILLE AIRSHIP

On May 6, 1897, near Hot Springs, Arkansas, a constable and deputy sheriff were riding toward the northwest at Blue Ouachita Mountains, just outside of Jessieville, to investigate a report of cattle rustling.

The pair spotted a bright light that shot across the sky and then disappeared behind the mountains. The men thought it odd but kept going. After another couple of miles of riding, the men saw the light again. This time, it was descending toward the mountains, but once again, it disappeared. The lawmen thought it was odd but kept going for another half mile. That's when their horses refused to move from fear of something off in the distance. They drew their guns and decided to investigate what was making the horses so skittish.

Off in the distance, the two officers saw three men wandering around, carrying lanterns. A man with a beard came forward and told the two lawmen that he and his companions were traveling across the country in an airship. The bearded men led the group to the craft, which was cigar-shaped and spanned about sixty feet. The traveler suggested the two men come on board the airship and take a look around, but they were too hesitant and declined. They went back to their horses and went on their way to search out the cattle rustling claims. Later in the evening, the officers returned to the same spot, and the airship with its mysterious travelers were gone.

The story circulated, but no one else in the area had a similar experience. There was a man in Hot Springs who applied but not did not receive a "flying machine" patent. He was known to have been experimenting with creating with some kind of craft, but nobody ever saw him with anything that actually worked.

A few months later, a man in Mississippi relayed a similar story of meeting a man with a lantern who showed him an airship.

THE HEALING SPRINGS
OF ARKANSAS

During the early 1800s, spiritualism started to gain momentum, and with it came a growing interest in the healing arts, tonics and faith cures. The railroad systems in the United States made travel affordable and gave the middle class access to wellness centers in remote forested locations.

Healing springs provided one of the most popular cures of the time, and promoters boasted access to the waters could remedy just about any malady, including tuberculosis, hay fever, asthma, jaundice, indigestion, gout, cancer and all menstrual issues. As technology advanced so did the properties of the healing springs. When electricity started to inhabit more homes, hotels and wellness centers, "magnetic" water became all the rage. The electricity allegedly magnetized the water, attracting metals that gave it more potent healing properties. In 1898, when Madame Curie discovered radium, the idea of "radioactive" water became en vogue, and travelers searched for places with this kind of healing spring.

The earliest health resort popped up in the United States in Saratoga Springs, New York, sometime in the early 1800s. The first bathhouse started running in Arkansas in Hot Springs in the early 1830s, and wellness centers were popularized in the Ozarks in the 1880s. Eureka Springs and Siloam Springs became the most popular of these areas in the state and housed numerous wellness centers. However, Siloam Springs quickly diminished because of the lack of railroad stops in the area. The age of medicinal water and healing centers lasted only until the early 1900s, when people started to rely more on western medicine and the advances in healthcare. But many still travel to the Ozarks to experience the healing properties of the springs today.

HOT SPRINGS

Hot Springs is located along the Ouachita River in the Central Ouachita Mountains. It's named after the forty-seven natural thermal water springs that flow out of the ground at 147 degrees Fahrenheit. These springs have long been associated with healing properties, especially by the Natives who inhabited the area.

Though the Quapaw were said to be on the land since around 12,000 BCE, there is no written account of them in association with the springs until the late 1700s. A French naval captain visited the area and remarked that the Natives intentionally frequented the area to bathe in the healing waters because the "native physicians…claim that they are so strengthening."

Local lore stated the thermal springs were considered a neutral area, and anyone in the vicinity could use them without any kind of backlash. The Caddo tribe were said to frequent the area and bathe in the healing waters often. In the waters, truces were made—at least temporary ones.

In 1818, the Hot Springs area was ceded to the United States as part of a treaty. As migrants moved west, the springs gained popularity, and by the 1830s, bathhouses were popping up, creating a small town of wellness. The first bathhouses were haphazardly built and crude, formed of wood and canvas perched around reservoirs on top of rock. They were a little more than large tents used for bathing.

Hot Springs was incorporated in 1851, and the settlement created a space for more permanent buildings. Much of the town's streets at the time were lined with bathhouses and small businesses. The baths had hot and cold water that was pumped in the basins by wooden troughs and placed into tanks. You could choose your water by pulling the appropriate rope. After taking a bath, patrons went into a special "vapor room," which was made up of a thermal pool with wooden slats about two inches apart covering it so that the steam filled up the room. After the vapor room, bathers went into another room, where they were splashed with cold water.

By the 1900s, word of mouth about the medicinal qualities of the hot springs in the vicinity had created a buzz, and travelers flocked to the area. During this time, electric trolleys and telephones were new amenities that eased the burden of traveling and made the area more accessible. To accommodate the town's newfound popularity, larger and more elaborate bathhouses were built that included areas for spa treatments.

Wellness centers that focused mainly on health popped up, including the Crystal Bathhouse and the Levi Hospital, which still runs today.

Unfortunately, the Crystal Bathhouse burned down in a 1913 fire in the tourist district.

In 1926, Mayor Leo McLaughlin turned Hot Springs into an "open town," which meant gambling was legal there. Many bathhouses catered to the new popular form of entertainment. The Southern Club hosted a slew of gangsters and became a notorious hangout for heavy-hitters like Lucky Luciano, Owney Madden and Al Capone. By the 1960s, gambling had gone underground after it became illegal again. But the bathhouses were still used for those purposes.

When the Vapors Casino was bombed in 1963, the tragedy spurred city officials to crack down on the illegal shenanigans running the town. Many casinos and bathhouses were closed down until the late 1980s. Despite the closures, the town still grew, and many of the original elaborate bathhouses are back up and running today. The following bathhouses are a few you can visit in the town's downtown tourist district.

Buckstaff Bathhouse

509 CENTRAL AVENUE
HOT SPRINGS, AR 71901
501-623-2308

This bathhouse has been in constant use since its opening on February 1, 1912, and is one of the best-preserved buildings in the area. It can house up to one thousand bathers per day.

Quapaw Bathhouse

413 CENTRAL AVENUE
HOT SPRINGS NATIONAL PARK, AR 71901
501-609-9822

This bathhouse is the conglomeration of two other bathhouses: the Horseshoe and the Magnesia. It opened in 1922 and had a variety of spa treatments, including baths, vapor rooms, showers, massages and electrotherapy. The building was closed in 1968 and then reopened for health services. It utilized only twenty of its original tubs. The services were geared toward physical therapy and hydrotherapy. The bathhouse was closed again in the mid-1980s and didn't reopen until 2008, after major renovations.

The Three Sisters Springs

The Three Sisters Springs is located at
the Lake Ouachita State Park.
EAGLE EYE ROAD
MOUNTAIN PINE, AR 71956

Just twelve miles outside of Hot Springs, the Three Sisters Historical Site lies in the Ouachita Mountains. John McFadden originally homesteaded the area in 1875, and the entrepreneur picked the area because he believed its natural pools of water had healing properties. It is said he named the property Three Sisters because he had three daughters.

The land changed hands a few times from 1883 to 1907, when W.M. Cecil and his partners started the development of McFadden's Three Sisters Spring Resort, which included the resort, cottages and a spring house. In later years, Cecil opened a bottling company called Worlds Wonder Water, which packed the spring water in bottles and sold it worldwide. The owner claimed each spring cured different maladies. In 1927, a bottle of water cost twenty-seven cents.

According to the placards on the individual springs:

The first spring healed Bright's disease; diabetes; dropsy; pus in the kidney, bladder and urethra; cystitis; an enlarged prostate gland; paralysis; stones in the kidney and other urinary troubles; changes of life and female irregularities; insomnia; anemia; high or low blood pressure; gout; hyperacidity; rheumatism; and arthritis.

The second spring healed chronic constipation, chronic indigestion, catarrh of stomach, excessive acid, gastritis, ulcerated stomach, poor assimilation and elimination, low blood pressure, gallstones and mucus colitis.

And the third spring healed high astringent, constipation, diarrhea, dysentery, cholera infantum and kindred troubles. A bath could be used for diabetic sores and eczema, granulated and sore eyes and catarrh of the head, nose and sinuses.

The property changed hands a few more times until the U.S. Army Corps of Engineers acquired it in 1951 as part of the Lake Ouachita construction project. The three springs are still free flowing but are now funneled into one stream through natural stone and then fed into Lake Ouachita.

EUREKA SPRINGS

Eureka Springs has a history steeped in lore, magic and the metaphysical. Originally known as Basin Spring, the area was considered venerated and a neutral ground for visiting Native tribes. The Osage were the main tribe who used the spring, but because it was a common area, many other tribes frequented the springs. Legend states that a Sioux princess had an eye affliction that caused her blindness. She bathed in the healing waters of Basin Spring, and within hours, her sight returned. For this reason, the water source was called the Indians' Healing Spring.

Having heard the story about the Sioux princess, in 1856, Dr. Alvah Jackson came to the medicinal springs to heal his own son's eye ailment. He is considered the first white person to "discover" the healing waters of the Basin Spring. During the Civil War, Jackson created Dr. Jackson's Cave Hospital to help cure soldiers who engaged in battle. After the war, the entrepreneur let go of his hospital and created a business where he sold a tonic called Dr. Jackson's Eye Water, which was very popular and sold well.

By the 1870s, other bottling companies had quickly been erected in the area, catering to the newly bustling city of tourists looking for instant cures. One of the more popular water companies was called Ozarka Water Company, and it eventually got bought up by the Perrier Company. Ozarka is still bottling water to this day. It is now owned by Nestlé, but the water comes mainly from Texas and has no affiliation with the healing waters of Arkansas.

The wellness aspect of the springs brought in those who had ailments and were enthralled by the stories of the medicinal waters. Bathhouses and spas sprang up downtown. Visitors used trolleys to drive up and down the small, steep streets.

Each spring healed different maladies. The following are some of the diseases the healing waters were said to cure: kidney troubles, liver disease, Bright's disease, stomach problems, indigestion, insomnia, dropsy, asthma, anxiety and women's problems. Incredible testimonials canvased newspaper articles about how the sickly visited the town to bathe in the springs and had miraculous recoveries. Most attributed their healing journeys to the entire environment of Eureka Springs, not just the waters itself. Most surmised it was the combination of the fresh air, beautiful woods and magic of the waters. Those who showed up and didn't get cured were thought to have showed up too late into their sickness for the springs to be able to completely heal them.

Springs in Eureka Springs

BASIN SPRING
4 SPRING STREET
EUREKA SPRINGS, AR 72632

This is the original spring the Natives in the area used as their neutral healing ground and what brought tourists to the city. It's located in the middle of downtown in Basin Spring Park.

Crescent Spring

192b U.S. 62-City Route
Eureka Springs, AR 72632

This spring is named after the crescent-shaped rock behind it. It's another spring that is famously known for its medicinal properties, and it was visited often by those needing healing. Now, the water source is covered by a gazebo.

Blue Springs

Blue Springs Heritage Center
1537 Co Road 210
Eureka Springs, AR 72632

This blue-colored spring dumps thirty-eight million gallons of water a day into a trout-filled lagoon. The lagoon flows into the White River and is said to be the purest water in the area. The blue spring is known for healing physical and emotional wounds. The Osage tribe considered it sacred ground. It was used as a trading post and meeting a place.

Grotto Spring

313-505 U.S. 62-City Route
Eureka Springs, AR 72632

This spring is located in the mouth of a small cave dug into the side of the mountain. Etched on a square plaque above the cave's opening are the words *Esto Perpetua*, which means "let it be perpetual" in Latin. The phrase implies the healing waters of the spring will flow forever. In order to witness the spring, you must walk down a series of stone steps that are stamped by the Freemasons' symbol. Inside, there is a little shrine that houses burning glass candles and other spiritual offerings. During the 1800s, the grotto spring was a popular stopping spot for those traveling on horseback and tallyho parties.

Calif Spring

95 SOUTH MAIN STREET
EUREKA SPRINGS, AR 72632

This spring is located downtown next to the Eureka Springs Historical Museum. Its healing waters are not as well known. However, it does house one of the few remaining stone structures used in town for "purifying" water. They didn't work, which is why they aren't used today.

Harding Spring

151 SPRING STREET
EUREKA SPRINGS, AR 72632

This spring is named after photographer Emmett Harding, who popularized the idea of taking a souvenir picture in front of the healing waters. He set up a little building near the spring, where he sold his photographs and other merchandise he created. The most famous healing of Eureka Springs occurred at this site. Twenty-one-year-old Jenny Cowan had been blind for seven years due to an illness. Originally, she went to the basin park springs because of their popularity and used the water for a few months. However, her vision never returned. Cowan didn't want to give up, so she went to the Harding Spring and used its water exclusively. On August 22, 1880, her sight came back, and out in the streets, she exclaimed, "I can see!" Word of her miraculous healing went viral, and it cinched Eureka Springs as a wellness epicenter.

Sweet Spring

7 PINE STREET UPPER SUITE
EUREKA SPRINGS, AR 72632

Also known as Spout Spring, this water source was originally located in the mountain above its present location. In 1885, the city decided to make the spring more accessible and created a round brick area near the heart of town. The locals called it Sweet Spring because of the pleasant taste of its water.

Magnetic Spring

Magnetic Spring is located on Magnetic Mountain, just below Christ of the Ozarks. If you use GPS, you will be taken directly to it, despite it having no formal address.
MAGNETIC DRIVE
EUREKA SPRINGS, AR 72632

This spring was said to cure addiction and drunkenness. It was very popular for this reason, and it was added to the prescriptions of many of the ill who were addicted to the cocaine, heroin and booze at the time. Besides its healing properties, the spring allegedly magnetized anything that passed through its waters.

SILOAM SPRINGS

Established in 1880, Siloam Springs grew quickly due to the claims of the healing springs that dumped into Sager Creek. A merchant named John Hargrove heard stories from a local doctor about some of his patients being healed by the spring on his property. The merchant decided to build a community around the healing waters. He named it Siloam City after finding the name in the book of John. It referred to an ancient healing water source from Jerusalem called Siloam Pool.

Hargrove collected testimonials from people in the area who had drunk from the spring and been cured of their malady. Soon, the stories flourished, and tourists were flocking to the new city to have their own experience.

Initially, the spring trickled from a rock table in a hill. In order to make the spring more appealing, Hargrove had a wall built into the table rock with a sign. The water was siphoned into three water troughs through spouts.

The following is an advertisement about Siloam Springs from 1885:

Siloam Springs, Benton County, is situated in Northwest Arkansas. Siloam and Twin Springs, discovered in 1880, are attractions of our city, on account of their peculiar curative mineral waters. This section abounds in numerous fine streams of water. Plenty of timber, good lime and sandstone for building. Has coal, lead and other mineral deposits. The Ozark region, in which Benton and Washington Counties are situated, is noted for growing fine fruits, such as apples, peaches, pears, plums, grapes and berries, of large size and excellent flavor, and have taken premiums at Kansas City, St. Louis and the World's Fair at New Orleans. Fruit culture, fruit canning and drying, farming and stock raising are the principal industries. Surveys have been made, and on the completion of railroads North, South, East and West, Siloam is destined to be an important commercial center and supply point. A mild and healthy climate, a happy medium between the severe cold of the North and the constant heat of the South, good society, churches and schools.

In 1897, the city tore down the wall and created a less elaborate brick retention wall. Nobody knows the exact reason for this, but it's theorized the new wall was more about practicality, as Sager Creek tended to flood the area.

In 1911, more topiary and landscaping, along with benches and stairs, were added to the surrounding area to give the spring a more appeal. Today, the 1897 wall still stands, with added stonework at the bottom used to fortify it. There are two troughs at the bottom of the wall so that visitors can access the water.

NATURAL FALLS STATE PARK

Dripping Springs

19225 EAST 578 ROAD
COLCORD, OK 74338

Natural Falls State Park is on the border of Arkansas and Oklahoma, just outside of Siloam Springs. The dripping springs consist of a series of waterways and a seventy-seven-foot-tall rushing waterfall that dumps into a small cove created by the side of a mountain. Ownership of the land dates to 1907, but the Native people in the area used it as a source of water and its plethora of caves for shelter. During the Civil War, soldiers from both sides used the ravines and springs as hiding places and places for respite. If a Union soldier spotted a Confederate soldier (or vice versa), they would simply walk the other way or take a new route and pretend it didn't happen. It was one of the only neutral areas in the region. There's a myth that the

Confederates hid a cache of gold underneath the falls and never came back to retrieve it because a group of Union soldiers had entered the area.

The park has changed hands throughout the years, but eventually, it was sold to the State of Oklahoma for preservation in the 1990s. The state created a national park in the area in 1997 to make sure all could enjoy the park. Today, the waterfall receives about one hundred thousand visitors a year.

Monte Ne

Rogers

Lynn Lane

Rogers, AR 72758

Monte Ne was a planned wellness community nestled in the Ozark woods of Arkansas. In its heyday, it housed two of the largest log buildings in the world, the first indoor swimming pool in Arkansas and the only presidential campaign in the state to date.

Though the community existed for over thirty years, it was never considered a success due to overspending and funding issues. Its founder, William "Coin" Harvey, had big ideas and big dreams. However, his creative nature superseded the money coming in. Harvey died in 1936, totally bankrupt. His resort property was divided into plots and sold off to pay his debts. In 1964, the remnants of the community and its structures were flooded by the inception of Beaver Lake.

William "Coin" Hope Harvey Had a Dream

Before Monte Ne, Harvey had created much wealth and success for himself. His wealth came from flipping real estate and silver mining in Colorado. He wrote a pamphlet that he sold titled *Coin's Financial School*, which delved into

the importance of an economic policy called "free silver" that advocated for the unlimited coinage of silver. Harvey wrote the pamphlet in 1893 and sold over two million copies. At the time, the only book to sell more copies was the Bible. The popularity of the pamphlet made Harvey one of the leading advocates for free silver in the United States. It gave him a lot of clout and political opportunities.

Before hitting it big, Harvey had law practice in Barboursville, West Virginia. Early on in his career, he took on a highly controversial case for the time. He defended a white man who married a Black woman, which was illegal in the state. He got the charges dismissed and gained enough influence to keep his practice busy for the next three years. In the next few years, Harvey moved to Ohio and Illinois, where he practiced law with his brother. In 1885, he quit his practice for health reasons and moved to Colorado.

In 1895, Harvey created his own political party known as the Patriots of America, which advocated for direct legislation and free silver. He used the platform to help campaign for the Democratic presidential electee William Jennings Bryan, who ran on a heavy silver-positive platform. Bryan lost to Republican candidate William McKinley, and the defeat took Harvey out of politics and into the remote woods of Arkansas.

While on the campaign trail, Harvey bought 5 acres in the Ozarks near Rogers, Arkansas. Then in 1900, he returned and purchased 320 more acres in a town called Silver Springs from a man named Reverend Bailey. The landowner moved into Bailey's old log cabin to prepare the land. In the following months, his son Tom moved into the cabin to help make preparations and renovations for the arrival of the rest of the family. Harvey's wife, Anna, and his two other children, Annette and Hal, eventually moved to Arkansas.

Unfortunately, shortly after the family was reunited, a fire started in the cabin, burning it down along with all of Harvey's possessions. Gutted by the loss, Anna, Annette and Hal decided to not stay in Arkansas and traveled back to Chicago, Illinois, where she initially lived before the move. She would only come back to Arkansas a few times for very short visits.

Harvey would end up making Arkansas his home. He was cited as saying he loved the state because there were no large cities in the area and there was a lack of wealthy people. At that point in his life, he was tired of politics and status. He wanted more out of life and had a vision of creating a wellness community on his land that mimicked the European health spas in larger cities.

The Inception of Monte Ne

When Harvey had the idea to create a resort and wellness center in Arkansas, he decided to change the name of the city from Silver Springs to Monte Ne. The post office was on board with the idea, since people regularly confused Siloam Springs and Silver Springs, causing all kinds of lost mail. Harvey used the words *monte*, which, in Spanish, means "mountain," and *ne*, the word for "water" in the Native language. He felt the name represented the most beautiful aspects of the area.

At first, Harvey spent his funding and time working on creating waterways for his new community. He hired Albert Graham to dredge a canal and build masonry abutments to form a floodgate that would move the waters of Elixir Spring and Big Spring into the newly created Big Spring Lake. He also improved on an already natural waterfall where two springs intersected by building a wooden and stonework bridge there. This way, visitors could sit and relax while viewing the moving waters.

Around the springs, Harvey built wooden walkways and small square wooden platforms so that tourists could picnic and gather at leisure. One of the amenities he supplied was drinking the spring water as a refreshment. If one didn't feel like walking around the springs, they could indulge in a gondola ride or utilize one of the small rowboats and enjoy the scenery that way.

In 1901, the entrepreneur started building three bridges that would become walkways from the hotels over what he called the lagoon to the lake parks and recreations areas. The lagoon consisted of the waterways that dumped into Big Spring Lake. There were two simple bridges that were twins of each other and one bridge in the middle that was more ornate with eight battlement piers. The bridges took four months in total to build.

The wellness center opened its doors on May 4, 1901, and consisted of one dwelling called Hotel Monte Ne. It was a three-story building with two three-hundred-foot-long wings. Each hotel room had an outside entrance with wide porches for visitors to gather and socialize. Meals were prepared in the dining room on the bottom floor on the east side of the building. The front of the hotel faced the lagoon, and visitors could get down to the water by a set of wooden stairs that took them to the gondolas and small rowboats. During its grand opening, the Hotel Monte Ne hosted a ball in the dining room. The exterior of the hotel was adorned with hundreds of Japanese lanterns.

Harvey spared no expense and even commissioned a tribute song for Monte Ne. Written by Edward Wolfe, the song "Beautiful Monte Ne" was copyrighted by Harvey in 1906. The chorus of the song goes like this:

Beautiful Monte Ne
God's gift to man, they say.
Health resort of the all the world is beautiful Monte Ne
Rosy cheeks and purer blood they gain there day by day.
In mountain air and water rare at beautiful Monte Ne.

TRANSPORTATION

With the popularity of Monte Ne on the rise, Harvey knew that transportation needed to be accessible for those traveling from other states. Arkansas, at the time, was very remote, and unless you were from the area or had transportation, the resort wasn't easy to find. Cars were still a luxury for the wealthy, and most people relied on trains for traveling.

The entrepreneur set out to fund a train stop at his resort and went to the surrounding cities for help. He spoke with leaders from both Rogers and Lowell. Rogers was not interested, but Lowell decided a train would be a great boost for the economy of the area and chose to help fund the project. The city donated a $250,000 bond to build the railroad.

With fourteen thousand oak wood railroad ties, Harvey had a private five-mile railroad track built that went from the Lowell transfer station to Monte Ne. Harvey built a log cabin–type building with an open waiting area at the south end of Big Spring Lake to be used as the private train station.

The train would drop visitors off at the train station. Then they would then be transferred to the Hotel Monte Ne by a gondola on the beautiful Big Spring Lake. Rides cost ten cents, and Harvey boasted that visitors would never have such an enchanting and unique experience anywhere in the world.

On June 19, 1902, the train stop officially opened. Harvey had a celebration that had a lower than predicted attendance, because it rained most of the day. However, locals did come out to witness the new transportation system and enjoy the resort. Harvey hosted a dance in the dining room, which was said to be a huge success, as people danced until well after 2:00 a.m.

MORE HOTELS

Harvey had a vision of building five hotels in total at Monte Ne. He wanted a giant three-story building that looked like a castle called the Club House Hotel, which would function as the main hub, and four smaller hotels that that were 300 to 450 feet long and had a row of cottage-style rooms. The smaller hotels were to be named after the states surrounding Arkansas.

In August 1904, the construction of the Missouri Row Hotel began. The completed building was 46 feet wide and 400 feet long. The two ends and the middle had second floors, and like the Hotel Monte Ne, they housed large 575-foot-long porches. Each room was described as being 16 feet square and included a fireplace. In September 1905, Missouri Row opened, and a room cost one dollar per day or six dollars per week.

In February 1907, Harvey began building his second hotel, called Oklahoma Row. It was set to the west of Missouri Row, and a large lawn spanned between them. The hotel had forty rooms equipped with a fireplace, electricity, sewerage and access to piped-in spring water. Oklahoma Row had a three-story cement tower on its south side that housed rooms, a dance hall in the center and a dining room on the north side. Like the other hotels, Oklahoma Row had long porches used for socializing during the day for admiring the good weather.

Oklahoma Row took longer to build because of its extra amenities and a shortage of cash flow. Harvey complained the 1907 season had been a failure and that he didn't get the number he needed to keep the books in the black. However, the entrepreneur was good at raising money, and by March 1909, Oklahoma Row opened its doors without a grand opening celebration. Rooms cost $2.40 a day or $10.00 per week, with meals costing $0.50. At the time, the two hotels were the largest buildings in the world.

MONTE NE AMENITIES

Across the street from the lagoon, Harvey's son and brother-in-law set out to create Arkansas's first pool. It was twenty-five feet wide, fifty feet long and seven feet deep. The water was dumped into the basin from the Silver Spring Creek. Half of the pool was sectioned off, and heated water was pumped in from a boiler pipe. The pool had a diving board, slides and individual dressing rooms. Access to the pool cost twenty-five cents, and an additional twenty-five cents was required for the use of bathing suits and a towel. At the other end of the pool house building, there was a two-lane bowling alley.

Aside from walking the woods and picnicking on the lake boardwalks, favorite pastimes at Monte Ne were fishing and foxhunting. The lake was regularly replenished with rainbow trout to make sure those who went fishing had a good chance of catching something. In 1908, the Fox Hunter's Association had its annual meeting and foxhunt. It attracted over one hundred people.

Harvey always wanted there to be a festive environment around Monte Ne. He hired bands from Fayetteville to play around the lake and lagoon. The resort hosted weekly dances in the hall that attracted locals. The booze flowed freely, and they were so popular, the newspaper wrote about their ensuing shenanigans.

The wide lawn between the Missouri Row and Oklahoma Row hosted lawn tennis and croquet. In 1908, the first golf course in Northwest Arkansas was placed just east of downtown Monte Ne. Being a fairly new sport, it was very significant for visitors to be able to play the premier game.

Downtown Monte had a bank, a post office and a slew of mercantile shops and boutiques. The local Oddfellows chapter used the top of the bank for its meetings. Harvey created his own scrip that could be used downtown so visitors at the resort didn't need to worry about carrying money.

The Downfall of Monte Ne and the Pyramid

Though Monte Ne was initially successful, the resort started to decline as the years went by, mostly due to Harvey's grandiose vision, his plunge into politics and his elaborate spending. By 1914, he had failed in his bid to represent the congressional district, even after spending hundreds of dollars on campaigning; the Monte Ne Railroad had been dismantled; and the Monte Bank had gone bankrupt. The resort itself still had consistent visitors but nowhere near the amount it had in its heyday.

In the 1920s, Harvey became jaded. His health was on the decline. The lack of funding and the series of failed ideas had started to whittle down his resolve. The entrepreneur felt the issues that plagued him stemmed from a broken political system that would eventually bring down the fall of society.

In 1927, he wrote a book called *Common Sense*, which highlighted his prediction of a catastrophe. He was sure the mountains around Monte Ne

would eventually crumble. His solution was to build an obelisk he called "the pyramid" that would function as a time capsule so that humanity had a starting point to repair itself. The pyramid would consist of an underground two-vault structure that housed Harvey's own books, the Bible, newspapers of the time and encyclopedias.

Preparing the land for the structure started in 1923. The pyramid was to sit at the south end of Big Spring Lake at an elevation to keep it from flooding. In 1925, Harvey started building a concrete retaining wall around the already-completed 40-foot-wide base of the pyramid. By 1928, the entrepreneur had begun the construction of what he called the terrace, stadium, foyer and entrance of the pyramid. In reality, he had built a large, semi-rounded amphitheater with benches for seating between five hundred and one thousand people. The structure stood around 20 feet tall and 140 feet wide.

Unlike other projects at Monte Ne, the pyramid had no preplanned design or blueprints. Harvey intuitively built the structure on and off for a number of years when he had the funding. After the amphitheater was built, the pyramid was supposed to be erected and attached to the righthand side of the structure.

During the construction phase, visitors to Monte Ne would meander to the amphitheater build to picnic and write their names in the concrete. Harvey found this to be tedious and decided to monetize the experience. He did this by constructing a portable wooden wall that hid the construction site. For twenty-five cents, onlookers could pass the wooden wall and watch Harvey oversee the pyramid build. He would talk to the paying customers about his vision, pass out a pamphlet about the pyramid and talk about his doomsday politics. He had a shelf with rows of his books for sale for those who were influenced by his pontification.

In 1928, Harvey dedicated the amphitheater in front of a crowd of about five hundred people. He delivered a speech about his ideas, and then a band played music. The story of his pyramid had been picked up by many newspapers around the country due to the new Egyptian craze. King Tut's tomb had been discovered in 1922, and the intrigue about the pyramids had reached a new height. Due to this, Harvey had over twenty thousand people visit the amphitheater in the four-month span after its dedication.

THE END OF AN ERA

The construction of the pyramid continued until 1929, when the stock market crashed. Harvey then shifted his attention to politics once again and created the Liberty Party in 1930. To promote his new political views, he started a newsletter called the *Bugle Call* and wrote a book simply called *The Book*, which highlighted the party's agenda.

In 1931, Harvey held the first and only presidential convention in Arkansas. In order to join the convention, delegates had to read *The Book* and agree to its political stance. The convention brought together 786 delegates, even though Harvey predicted thousands might come.

During the convention, Harvey was elected as the presidential candidate for the Liberty Party. After rigorous campaigning, he came in fifth place, and Franklin Roosevelt became the president of the United States. After losing the election, Harvey continued to be political and sell copies of his book. He would regularly write about how he had disdain for Roosevelt's silver policies in a newsletter called the *Liberty Bell*.

By 1935, Harvey's health had started to decline, and he had lost most of his sight. He died at the age of eighty-four on February 11, 1936, of intestinal influenza at his home in Monte Ne. While his body was at the funeral home, awaiting to be buried, a death mask was made of his face. You can view the mask at the Rogers Historical Museum.

After Harvey's death, Monte Ne faded away. Oklahoma Row and Missouri Row were used for lodging but changed hands many times. People still came to see the amphitheater, but it was more of a local spectacle and not associated with the pyramid project. By the mid-1940s, Coin Harvey and his dream had long been forgotten. His vision no longer existed, and Monte New became nothing more than a memory.

WHAT'S LEFT OF MONTE NE?

Most of the buildings from Monte Ne are now underwater. The resort town was in the path of flooding when the White River Basin was dammed in the 1960s to create Beaver Lake. Parts of the bridges and the amphitheater were dismantled to keep boats from running into them. The concrete chairs that were placed in the apex of the amphitheater were removed and placed in the Rogers Historical Museum. When the lake falls under 111 feet, the tops of the amphitheater and retaining wall peak out from water. It's common for divers to explore the submerged buildings and witness what's left of the wellness town.

On land, some of the foundation and retaining wall of Missouri Row are still somewhat intact. Pieces of the original stairs and a chimney tower are the most notable relics. Chunks of concrete are strewn among the woods. There's a boat drop-off just past Missouri Row that used to be the foundation for the clubhouse hotel that was never finished. If you look closely, you will notice pieces of concrete on the ground.

As of February 2023, the foundation, tower and concrete basement of Oklahoma Row were demolished and no longer exist. Parts of the tower were taken to the Rogers Historical Museum. The original hotel rooms and the Monte Ne Train Station sit on a private piece of property just off the highway. The buildings are shoddy and in disrepair. The wood is deteriorating, and the buildings slant from having no real foundation.

Harvey's tomb stands on a piece of private property just past the ruins.

THE GHOST OF MONTE NE: DEAR DARLA

Here's how the story goes. In 1998, Darla Johnson and her boyfriend Jason headed out to the Monte Ne ruins for a lake party. The pair started drinking inside of the dilapidated tower of the old Oklahoma Row. After becoming inebriated, Darla and Jason went off by themselves for some alone time. While they were making out, a man dressed in all back attacked the boyfriend from behind. Darla struggled away from the situation and turned to run toward the highway, screaming for help. The perpetrator ran after the teenager to silence her. Around this time, the other partygoers heard Darla's screams and went toward where the attack happened. They saw the man run away in the woods toward the girl.

Shocked and afraid, the teenagers stayed where they were and wondered what to do. The screams of Darla kept them frozen in place. Then, suddenly, the screaming stopped, and the man never came back. The teenagers waited for a while to make sure they weren't in danger. Then they left the ruins and went to a payphone to call the police. According to the story, the police searched the highway and the side of the road. The lake was dredged, and the surrounding woods were canvassed, but Darla's body was never found.

The ghost of Darla is said to haunt the area around the Monte Ne ruins. People have claimed they saw a screaming teenage girl running from the woods near the highway. Others have witnessed a shadowy figure staring down at them from the third floor of the tower of the old Oklahoma Row.

The eeriest interaction with Darla is much more interactive and leaves people in a state of terror and confusion. It's said that the teenager just wants to go home. She will walk toward your car and ask for a ride. If you say yes, she will get into the passenger side, give you the directions and then not say anything for the entire ride. Once you get to her house and turn to tell her she's home, she will disappear like she was never there in the first place.

According to a post from October 2010, his happened to a man who picked up the teenage ghost. But this time, she had a sweater. The only thing she said to the driver was, "My mom said this was her favorite sweater on me."

The man turned to say something to the girl, but she had disappeared—leaving her sweater behind. Feeling uneasy about the situation, the man took the sweater to the door of the address the teenager had given him. He asked the woman who answered the door if someone in the house owned the sweater. The woman broke down and fell to her knees. She explained the sweater belonged to Darla and that she was still missing.

Darla is mostly seen and experienced in the last couple of weeks of October. If you do visit Monte Ne and you see a teenage girl on the side of the road, proceed with caution. She's not a dangerous ghost, but she's also not really there.

THE AUTHOR'S EXPERIENCE AT MONTE NE

I've lived in Arkansas for a total of four years. I moved from Tucson, Arizona, and stayed for two years. Then I moved back to my hometown in Southern California for two years before coming back to Arkansas. As of this writing, I am nearing my second year in Arkansas. This time, I bought a house in the area, so there's a good chance I will be laying down roots in Northwest Arkansas.

Both times I've lived in the Natural State, I've heard about Monte Ne. It's one of those odd pieces of trivia the locals talk about and don't think much of. One time, the tower and the lake made it on the cover of one of the local magazines. It had an article about the town and its origin story. I held on to the magazine for a little while, thinking I would get to read it, but I never did. On one of my cleaning sprees, it ended up in the trash.

So, it's weird that I ended up at the Monte Ne ruins on a blustery, wet and rainy day. I walked through puddles and tried to keep the raindrops from pelting my glasses just to get a sight of what was left of the health resort. I had a compulsion to see it, and now I know that in just a couple of months, the concrete structure and the tower would be nothing more than a memory to locals.

I had gone to breakfast with my friend Kelli and another woman I had just met. We talked for hours at breakfast and then went to the other woman's house to finish up the conversation. There, the three of us got into a conversation about ghost towns. Monte Ne was mentioned because it was only fifteen minutes away, but because the weather was about to get stormy, nobody wanted to risk going to see it. We opted to have an adventure at another time. However, I am impatient, and like I said before, I had this strange compulsion. So, I punched the name into Google Maps, and it instantly showed up.

When I parked my car, I immediately stepped into a puddle. My shoes were drowned in water, and my socks were soaked. I pressed on, however, and walked toward the looming three-story tower covered in the bold colors of years of graffiti. Before it got torn down, it was fenced off with a slit on the lefthand side just large enough for a person to fit through. Clearly, the fence did nothing to guard against trespassing.

I was lucky that day, because the water for Beaver Lake was low. Usually, parts of the tower are underwater, and you can't walk a full 360 degrees around it. On that day, I didn't trespass and go inside the tower building, because I had a weird feeling wash over me. The tower has no windows left, just the square openings where they should be. I looked up at the third floor and felt something looking down at me. I muttered to myself, "This place is probably haunted."

I knew I would probably find a ghost story associated with the third floor, and I didn't want to face the building alone if, in fact, my intuition was correct. I was too tired and didn't know what I was getting myself into. This is one of the only times I didn't go full force into something without thinking about it. Maybe I was just cold.

The wind picked up, and I felt it was time to leave. So, I took some photographs and videos and then headed back to my car. Little did I know that the concrete slab I walked across to get to the tower was actually the base foundation for Oklahoma Row, and during the summer, when the lake is at its peak, it's used as a place to put kayaks into the water. However, in the winter, the lake is low, and you can go underneath into what people consider the basement, which had a maids' quarters, complete with a fireplace.

I didn't get to experience that cool little detail until I met Kelli at the ruins, and she showed me the rest of Monte Ne that I did not know even existed. We went into the Oklahoma Row basement area and found sigils spray-painted on the walls. With some research, Kelli found out that the sigils and symbols had to do with a summoning ritual. We kind of laughed it off, thinking it was a bunch of kids trying to do stupid things because they were bored. However, upon talking to some other locals, I found out that the Monte Ne ruins are known to be the place where the esoteric-minded went to do dark rituals and conjure demons.

Is that just local folklore, or is it reality? One will never know. The sigils and symbols we encountered show that something is going on there, but we will never know if it was actually used or if it was placed there to perpetuate the myth. Luckily, Kelli and I are experienced practitioners and don't get spooked easily. We only experienced amusement and some mild curiosity.

The ruins of the Missouri Row are just a short walk away. It takes less than five minutes to get to the other side of the lake. There's not a lot left of the second hotel. There's a retaining wall that goes to some stairs that probably went up to the front of the hotel. There are giant chucks of concrete and pieces of the building strewn about in the woods.

A chimney tower that housed fireplaces for at least two stories still stands. It also has a ton of graffiti on it. The outline of the rooms on the first floor of Missouri Row can be faintly seen in the dirt. There are still bricks in the ground that create the perimeters of different rooms.

We were very lucky the day we went to the ruins because the water of Beaver Lake was under 111 feet. The tops of the retaining wall and part of the amphitheater peeked out of the water. On the other side of the lake, we could see another part of the ruins that looked like a possible canal that went into the lagoon. We weren't totally sure though because the lake barely gets down low enough to see what is there. The last time the water in Beaver Lake was low enough for visitors to walk on the amphitheater was in the 1970s during a time of drought.

Since then, parts of the structure and the bridges have poked out of the water. Some of the locals told me that the water level of the lake had to be raised because people kept scraping the bottoms of their boats. There's a story about how there was piece of the amphitheater that stood up almost like an obelisk. Someone ran their boat into it, and it broke off. I'm not sure if the story is true, but I do know that the lake depths have been raised a few times throughout the years.

The last thing Kelli and I discovered was the grave of Coin Harvey. When Beaver Lake was being formed, his grave was near his house in Monte Ne. It was moved so that it wouldn't be underwater. Now, the square white sepulcher sits on a small patch of private land next to someone's home. It's a really weird place to have a grave marker. We stood by it, put our hands on it and said our goodbyes to Harvey and thanked him for creating such a cool space. We told him his vision was definitely not forgotten.

Kelli and I went to Monte Ne one last time. In February 2023, we found out that the tower and Oklahoma Row were going to be demolished because they had been deemed too hazardous for the community. Most of the time, the basement was underwater, and the tower was partly submerged. I'm not sure why it was considered dangerous all of a sudden. I did try to do research on the subject but hit a lot of walls.

All I got was that the Rogers Historical Museum was involved, since, technically, the ruins are considered a historical location. Those are supposed to be kept intact. However, instead of keeping the physical ruins, they were going to put up a plaque with a picture of the landmark.

Kelli and I went to the ruins the day before the demolition date. To our surprise, we weren't the only ones there. Many of the locals came out to say goodbye to the structure. Many were talking to each other about their memories of their time at the ruins. We heard stories about playing in the amphitheater before the flooding of Beaver Lake. A couple of people told us that there was a rope next to a tree that stood near the tower. The kids in the area would climb to the second floor and then use the rope to swing and drop into the lake water. These were beautiful tales steeped in nostalgia.

Kelli and I said our goodbyes and took a small piece of concrete from the tower to commemorate the time we spent there. It was a bittersweet moment leaving the area, knowing that it would be the last time the tower stood. I am grateful that I got to experience the remnants of Coin Harvey's dream.

He was a visionary and a leader. The entrepreneur had a reputation for being moody and difficult. He was the kind of person you either loved or hated. However, he did dare to dream. Sometimes, he had great success, and sometimes, he failed. But at the heart of Monte Ne was the desire to create something magical and life changing.

I believe Harvey created that, and even though Monte Ne is no longer standing, it will never be forgotten. It will live on in the memories of those who got to witness it firsthand and who got to play on its ruins, not realizing its history. It is a beautiful, idyllic piece of Northwest Arkansas history.

KELLI'S EXPERIENCE AT MONTE NE

There are many words to be said about the drowned ghost town that is Monte Ne. Of all the dead towns I've visited, I've never met one underwater.

William Coin Harvey predicted a catastrophic event resulting in death. He was definitely tapped into something, as Monte Ne has died three times. First, in its financial life, it ceased to be the booming town and resort imagined by its creators. Second, it was drowned in the flooding of White River, which is now part of Beaver Lake. And third, it was recently laid to rest by the Arkansas Corps of Engineers.

This is a place that has been between life and death for almost one hundred years. With notes of occultism in its beginnings, it's no wonder there are still signs of it being used in practices today. From pyramids to visions and a multitude of healing spring waters, Monte Ne was built in a time when spiritualism and connection to the other side was a normal part of life. It was no real surprise to find that modern magicians in the area had also taken note of the incredible energy source residing in the hills here.

Beneath the concrete slab of the main floor lies the hollow remnants of the old staff quarters. These rooms would become completely exposed in lower lake levels and fully submerged in high months, this swelling and falling of the water acting almost like a battery to any magical workings left in these little man-made caves. Bright green spray paint brought to life the sigil workings for the lake to charge and its sacred waters to carry away. Standing within the rooms of these surprisingly solid structures, one feels similar to how they would feel in a cave. Being nestled into the Earth, there is grounding and safety. It feels special and much like you are merely a visitor to this hidden pocket in the Earth.

Monte Ne has a special kind of sadness to it, a dream dead and forgotten and an entire town so lost to time that portions were put to rest beneath a lake. For one hundred years, it has been slowly dying, the last standing structure of the original town being a small piece in a series of hotel rows that served the many people who came to experience the profound beauty of the Ozarks. With so much love for the area and its history, I find it sad that the tower sat there alone on the shoreline, overlooking the bones of its brother next door.

The dead town of old Monte Ne is now submerged beneath the water. Some days in the dry of winters, it might get lucky enough to catch a glimpse of the amphitheater that was meant to house a large pyramid with the main objective of commemorating the coming fall of Monte Ne.

In modern times, lake life is a welcomed calm in an ever moving and increasingly loud society, but for Monte Ne, this is a downgrade from the original serenity of the Ozark hills. The once peaceful, spring-filled valley is now home to a cacophony of boat motors. As with all things, time brings change and new generations of life and priorities.

Regardless, this place remained for so long and still carries that lingering liminal space energy. For almost one hundred years it lay dying slowly, watching pieces of itself fall to the elements and waiting for its death. I believe Heather and I to be receivers of a distress call, calling to any bone collectors who appreciate the strange life and times of this unique town of the Ozarks.

If you visit the old site, you can feel the power still lingering in the winds and the waves. You can still visit Harvey's tomb and pay tribute to this very interesting and complex man who built an equally interesting and complex entity that is Monte Ne. The amphitheater itself deserves an entire book written for its purpose and life.

For now, the resort as a whole will forever live on in our hearts and in the stories of the drowned ghost town at the bottom of a lake. Rest in Peace, Monte Ne. We give thanks for the joy and expansion you brought to so many people who were eager to experience your natural beauty and strange personality.

PART II

SUPERNATURAL STRANGENESS

Strange Lights in Arkansas

The Dover Lights

Old Highway 7
Dover, Arkansas

The Dover Lights were first observed in the 1800s and are still a mysterious phenomenon to this day. Many people theorize the lights are related to automobiles or electricity. However, the oddity started showing itself before either were staples in everyday life.

To see the lights, you need to take Old Highway 7, twelve miles outside of the city limits, to an overlook above Big Piney Creek. The site is located higher up on a mountain, so you can see the whole valley below. Any time after dusk, after the sky gets dark, and with a little luck, you may get a glimpse of the lights. It doesn't have a schedule—it happens when it wants to.

The lights show up as round reddish or gold orbs that flicker on the ground. Sometimes, they dance in the sky, moving back and forth at lightning speed, only to return to the ground. They tend to stay in the same area, even when they move in the sky. You may see the phenomenon more than once throughout the night. It seems to stop and start when it wants, and some have said it responds to other lights, including lightning.

There are many folklore stories associated with the lights, though no one has been able to figure out what they are or how they are made. Some believe there was a mine in the valley that collapsed and that the lights are specter

carbine lanterns from the miners who lost their lives and who want to make sure they aren't forgotten.

Another story tells the tale of ghostly Spanish conquistadors searching the valley for gold. The lights move when the spirits change locations, digging for treasure. Locals have said if you yell "I've got your gold!" through the valley, it will "wake up" the lights and get them to flicker. The spookiest story says the valley is an old Native burial ground, and the lights are tribal leaders showing their dead the way to the other side.

The most detailed story is about an elderly couple who lived outside of town in the valley. The wife became ill, and the husband rode into town to find a doctor. He met a younger doctor who felt for the couple and spent the next few days nursing the wife back to health. For payment, the husband gave the doctor twelve homemade rifle bullets, since he didn't have much money.

A couple of years went by, and the doctor thought nothing of the transaction until he ran into the bullets while cleaning. He decided to put the bullets on display in his office to honor a time when he wasn't as successful and helped people for nearly nothing. While cleaning the bullets, he realized they were not made of lead but of pure silver.

The doctor became greedy, thinking that perhaps the elderly couple had confused silver with lead. Instead of telling the couple of their riches, he devised a plan to go back to their house to try to find where the man was getting the silver.

When the doctor went back to the couple's home, he didn't find them there. Instead, he found gravestones on the property. The couple had died long ago, but their house and property remained. He assumed there must be a silver mine nearby where the husband had made the bullets.

He took a lantern and went looking around but found no mine. He did find a crate with some silver bars in it behind the house. He took a couple and put them in his pocket and then vowed to come back in the morning with a horse to pack the rest of the silver. Unfortunately, the doctor died in his sleep. The lights are said to be the elderly couple retracing the steps of the doctor, trying to find the silver he stole.

In 2009, an amateur myth-buster named Daniel Cruse scoured the valley looking for the source of the Dover Lights. He was sure they were a fabricated hoax. After buying hundreds of dollars' worth of equipment, he went out with his partner and drove around, looking for clues.

Near a popular swimming spot, he saw what seemed to be an emergency warming blanket stretched across the ground. Upon further inspection, he realized it was a three-layer roll of aluminum foil spread four to five feet wide. A tiki torch was stuck in the ground at each corner. Clause believes the lights are just reflections of the torches bouncing off the silver foil or misidentified campfires.

Just like with the electricity and car theories, the Dover Lights have been around longer than foil and tiki torches. The lights will continue to be a mystery, and people will continue to drive up the old highway to hopefully spot them. They will have a cool supernatural story to share with their friends, and the folklore will live on.

The Gurdon Lights

151 AR-7
Gurdon, Arkansas

This is the most interesting light in Arkansas, in that its mystery is not centered on whether it exists but *why* it exists. It's a phenomenon that started in 1931 and has been readily photographed throughout the years. In 1994, the television show *Unsolved Mysteries* came to the small town of Gurdon to document the origins of the light.

Gurdon is about seventy-five miles outside of Little Rock on Highway 30 along a stretch of railroad tracks. Stop at the railroad tracks and walk down them until you cross over four creek bridges. If you want more specific directions, stop at any gas station. All of the locals know about it, and they call it the "ghost light bluffs."

You can't see the light from the highway. You have to hike two and a half miles and pass two trestles before you reach an area where you can witness it. You will know you are in the right place when the tracks slightly incline. The light seems to only show up during the darkest of nights or when it's overcast. It's an orangish or white light that hovers on the horizon. Sometimes, it sways back and forth.

Like most of the strangeness in Arkansas, the Gurdon Light is steeped in local folklore. However, there is a story associated with the phenomenon that's true. In 1931, a railroad foreman named William McClain fired a worker name Louis McBride (sometimes spelled McBryde). An angry McBride killed McClain for a reason that is unclear. Some say the worker caused a derailment from a piece of sabotaged track. Others speculate that McBride asked for more hours, and the foreman wouldn't give them to him. In either case, McClain was brutally beaten with a railroad spike maul. The railroad worker was sentenced to death by electrocution and died on July 8, 1932.

Due to this event, many locals believe the light is McClain walking his usual route with the lantern he used for work. Another twist on this same tale is a little more gruesome. It states that a local railroad worker went outside of town for the evening. When he came back, he accidentally fell in front of a train, and his head was severed from his body. They say the light is the headless man with a lantern searching the area for his head.

Many have tried to explain the light and figure out its origin. The easiest explanation states the light is just misidentified headlights from cars moving across the highway. However, debunkers suggest the light has been seen way before the highway was even there. So, it's not the source of the phenomenon.

In the 1980s, there were two different studies of the Gurdon Light. The first was done by a former graduate student from Henderson State University. According to an article from the *Arkansas Gazette*, the grad student stated, "The nearest interstate to the tracks is about four miles away, and a large hill stands in between the tracks and the interstate. If the light was caused by passing headlights, it would have to be refracted up and over the hill to be visible on the other side."

The second study was done by a professor of physics at Henderson State University. His specialty was the study of light. The professor found that the Gurdon Light never polarized, even when viewed through lenses. It never had any kind of electromagnetic current and showed up during all kinds of atmospheric conditions. This meant the light couldn't have come from any man-made source like a car.

There is another theory that suggests the light is of a natural origin called the piezoelectric effect. This effect happens when quart crystal underground gets squeezed together by the Madrid Fault, which passes through Gurdon. The squeezing emits a spark of light, and that's what people are seeing.

This could be the cause of the Gurdon light, but it is strange that the phenomenon started the same year as the killing of the railroad foreman. Whether you believe in the supernatural story or the effect of quartz crystal on the ground, the light still exists. If you experience the light, just hope you don't run into the train worker looking for his head.

The Crossett Spook Light

Ashley Road 425
Crossett, Arkansas

Take Highway 52 to the airport and turn left on Ashley County Road 17. The road curves sharply to the right and turns into Ashley 425. Continue north until the road turns to gravel. After a mile, you will pass the old deer camp on the right. There is an old chimney on the grounds. After the camp, there is an intersection between Ashley 425 and Ashley 16. When you see the intersection, turn around and drive back one hundred to two hundred yards.

Just outside of Crossett, Arkansas, people have seen a light coming off the railroad tracks since the early 1900s. The light changes color from white to red to blue and floats two or three feet above the ground. Sometimes, it floats in the trees or wobbles from side to side. The most interesting part of the Crossett Light and what sets it apart from other spook lights is that if you try to get close to it, it will disappear and then reappear at the same distance. The phenomenon has always been elusive but also intriguing.

Like the Gurdon Light, the main legend says there was a railroad worker who was decapitated in a strange train accident. The light is said to be the man wandering the area, searching for his head with a lantern. Some have said it's his wife who is holding the lantern. Others who have seen the light suggest that it's extraterrestrial in nature, maybe some kind of beacon to announce the presence of aliens.

One of the more interesting aspects of the Crossett Light is that it seems to affect car engines. There have been stories of people parking their cars to watch for the spook light. It will show itself, and then the cars won't start until it's gone. Locals say if you want to ensure the light shows up, turn your headlights on and off three times. Others have seen it even when they haven't performed the superstitious ritual. However, it never hurts to try it.

Skeptics go for the usual explanation, which is the highway nearby. However, like with most spook lights, the highway didn't exist when the first sightings of the light were documented. Another explanation that comes up frequently is that the light is the result of swamp gas. However, the phenomenon tends to happen during all kinds of weather and conditions. Fog or gas emitted from the ground could play a factor in when it appears, but it doesn't seem to be the source of the lights.

The Crossett Light started to appear when the railroad came into the area. The building of the tracks might have been a contributing factor to the phenomenon. Like with the Gurdon Light, the railroad may have helped set off the piezoelectric effect because of the large quartz crystal deposits in the area.

THE MENA POLTERGEIST

In 1961, Ed and Birdie Shinn lived in a farmhouse on Ransome Road, just three miles outside of the small quiet town of Mena, Arkansas. For fifteen years, they lived in the house and led a very mundane, simple life until their teenage grandson Charles moved in. Just a few months after the change, weird things started to happen.

Shortly after midnight, the windows in the Shinn house started to rattle. Ed got up to see what was causing the sound, but he found nothing of interest and went back to bed. A short time later, the couple heard knocking sounds on the walls and couldn't get back to sleep. This happened for weeks at a time, and the noises would change intermittently. Sometimes, instead of the knocking or rattling noises, they would hear a buzzing that sounded like someone using a handsaw in the middle of the night.

According to Shinn, one night, the sounds got so bad that he pleaded with the source to please go to sleep. In a weird turn of events, the entity or whatever was creating the disturbance answered by saying, "I don't sleep."

The wife was surprised by the reply and pleaded with the entity to let her sleep. It replied, "You don't need to sleep either."

The elderly couple were understandably freaked out and suffered in silence. They didn't tell anyone about strange nightly activity for fear that no one would believe them—or worse, the town would make them a subject of mockery.

For a year, the Shinns tried to keep the phenomenon to themselves, even though it continually escalated. The loud noises turned into kinetic activity.

Light bulbs unscrewed themselves out of their sockets and crashed to the floor. Utensils flew into the air. Matches would drop to the floor and ignite, starting small fires. Chairs and small pieces of furniture would move across the floor of the living room.

Charles's marbles would end up scattered around the room. He would clean them up and then leave, only to have them scatter again. A few times, Birdie got hit in the head by flying marbles as they were picked up and tossed around the living room. At night, the teenager would complain the entity would pull the covers off of him and leave him freezing in the middle of the night.

In some accounts, Ed is the one who accidentally let the secret slip, and in others, it's Birdie. However, on all accounts, it's the butcher Alvin Dilbeck who heard the story of the poltergeist activity and talked about it to locals. He stated that he didn't talk about it because of its salaciousness but because he was genuinely worried about the older couple. He initially asked someone to visit the farmhouse to make sure everyone was okay.

However, the news quickly spread, and the rumors started to fly around like the furniture in the Shinn house. Visitors started showing up to the property, hoping to witness the poltergeist activity. They would knock on the door and ask to tour the home. Even if they didn't experience anything, they would make things up. Stories started to circulate about the mailbox randomly levitating and rotating on its own. Coal buckets and dog food cans were said to levitate. Basically, anything attached to the house ended up being haunted for the looky-loos who wanted to have a paranormal experience.

Trespassing incidents and barn break-ins started to happen regularly, and finally, Shinn decided to call the police. Sherriff Scoggin and two deputy officers started to protect the property and keep the trespassers at bay. One night, the three men, along with four reporters, decided to stay at the house in the hopes of experiencing the phenomenon for themselves, thinking it might be some kind of prank. The Shinns and Charles stayed at their neighbor's house for safety. The house was quiet that night, and nothing seemed to happen except for lack of sleep.

After the dud night, Scoggin surmised the poltergeist activity had to be something more mundane. Shinn started to blame the happenings on the Cold War. He said in a newspaper article he thought the activity in his house could be from some kind of radioactive experiment that the government was covertly performing. His neighbor suggested it could be from uranium.

Scoggin had a different idea, however. He went down to the local high school and interrogated Charles about the phenomenon and whether he was involved. After some pushback, the teenager broke down and confessed he was the one behind the poltergeist activity. It all started because he felt his grandparents were too grumpy and were giving him a hard time. He said he used a pair of pliers and knocked them against his bedframe to make the knocking noises. He rattled the windows and rearranged the furniture when his grandparents were outside of the house. The teenager threw the marbles at his grandma's head, and when his grandparents were in the house, he would throw furniture from one room into the other to make it seem like things were moving. While the elderly couple were sleeping, he would sneak in and pull the covers down and then go into his own room to pretend like it had happened to him as well.

The teenager said he started the poltergeist activity to get back at his grandparents, but then the town found out about it, and he had to keep going with it to appease the new interest. He had been trying to figure out a way to stop. Charles ended up writing a formal apology for the newspaper, and eventually, the family moved out of the farmhouse. However, many people in Mena and surrounding areas didn't believe the confession. They thought Charles took the rap for the poltergeist phenomenon to quiet the interest and give some reprieve to the family.

To this day, people aren't sure whether the poltergeist activity existed. Skeptics suggested it would take an awful lot of preparation and stealth for Charles to have moved around the house without being seen, especially when pulling the covers off his grandparents in the middle of the night. But then others have suggested the Shinns were in their seventies and maybe weren't the best at paying attention. So, maybe he was able to do more right in front of them without them even realizing it.

Whether the Mena poltergeist is true or just the shenanigans of a moody teenager, the story has held over time. It's made an indelible imprint on the culture of a small Arkansas farm town.

PART III

GHOSTS AND GHOUL

THE EXPELLED

HUNTSVILLE

According to the website The Expelled, the haunted attraction was started in 2012 with a fifteen-thousand-square-foot space, ten volunteers and one month to put something together. Now, it has a ten-thousand-square-foot space and over fifty employees, and they spend weeks putting together over twenty-five terrifying installations. The haunted house has won a handful of awards throughout the years, including becoming the Number One Must See Scare in Arkansas in 2018.

The Expelled closed for two years during the COVID pandemic shutdown and had its reopening during the 2022 Halloween season. Even though the ghosts in the haunted house are largely manufactured, the location has had its fill of real-life tragedies that have created some intriguing paranormal phenomena.

In 1922, the building housed an illegal speakeasy. During a raid, a fight between patrons broke out, and an eighteen-year-old man was killed. His ghost is supposed to haunt the location.

In the seventies and eighties, the property was a slaughterhouse called Huntsville Locker Plant. The story says a thirty-four-year-old man fell into a meat grinder and died. People report hearing random screams in the building when no one is around.

During modern times, is it said a fifty-three-year-old woman was driving down old Highway 23 when she lost control and crashed. During the crash, she was ejected from her truck. Her body landed on the property. People have seen her wandering around, confused and looking for her truck.

In the last few years, people have spoken of an elderly woman who wandered from her home on the coldest night of the year. She fell into a kudzu pit and froze to death. Her body was found next to the haunted house property. She is also seen stumbling down the highway, looking dazed.

THE FEE HOUSE

LITTLE ROCK

1900 BROADWAY STREET
LITTLE ROCK, AR 72206

The Fee House is over 130 years old. It was originally built by Sebastian Virgil Hafer in 1892, but the misfortunes didn't come until later. The Fees were the third family to own the house and the most memorable. Even in the years after they left the home and others inhabited it, the Fees lingered.

In 1907, Frank Fee and his wife, Mamie, moved into the two-story house with their three children, all of whom were from Fee's first marriage.

Fee was a successful lumberman and a thirty-second-degree Mason who had memberships to most of the high-end social clubs. However, he was not without scandal. The lumberman had started an affair with Mamie while both were still married to other people.

The pair were the hot gossip in their social circle while people speculated about whether they were having an affair and sleeping together. It was even more salacious when the pair quickly divorced their spouses and, within a few months, had already remarried and moved in together.

The scandals didn't stop there. Mamie was pregnant twice while living in the house. She had a son named Thomas and a little girl named Patricia. When Thomas was born, there were rumors about who fathered him. Many believed Mamie had slept with a grounds person who lived in the carriage house.

The Fees largely ignored the rumors, since they were used to people talking about their business. However, there were clues in the household that showed

perhaps the rumors were true. The children had large bedrooms upstairs, except Thomas, who lived in a room behind the library on a sun porch. As soon as the boy was of high school age, he was sent off to California, where he stayed through college and his adulthood.

Out of all the Fees, his fate was possibly the luckiest. The other family members eventually died in strange twists of tragedy. It started with Frank in 1922. When he was on a business trip in Michigan, he had a fatal heart attack at the age of sixty-two.

Nine years passed before another tragedy rocked the family. In 1931, Mamie Fee, who was fifty-six at the time, had a strange accident in her dressing room. Patricia Bell, who is the granddaughter of Mamie, wrote this in an email:

> *We had an open grate (for heating the room) and my grandmother had washed her hair and she was in her nightgown drying her hair, over the stove—her gown caught fire—the made* [sic]*, Amelia, was the only one with her—she rolled her in a blanket, to smother the flames. She was burned—she would tell no one. Edward was to be married at that time, and she didn't want to spoil his marriage plans, so she kept her plight to herself. After the wedding she got so bad, she did go to a hospital, for the burns, but it was too late. From this she died. She was a good Christian Scientist—many the time she would call someone to pray that I would get well. Maybe that, too was a reason she didn't go to the hospital sooner.*

The distraught family tried to put the pieces back together after Mamie's death, but there was obvious tension between the brothers and their sister. In 1932, less than a year after their stepmother's death, Fee's eldest daughter, Katherine, died after drinking poison at the age of twenty-eight. The details of her death are suspicious, and there are different versions about what happened.

Here's what Patricia Bell had to say about the incident:

> *After the shock of Mamie's death, the family was clearly distraught. Less than a year later in 1932, daughter Katherine, age 28, died by drinking poison. The newspapers reported this horrific death as a "mistake," claiming Katherine said she had a headache while she, her husband, and two of her brothers were playing cards in the parlor. The official story is that in her attempt to take some medicine to relieve her headache, she inadvertently drank acid. She was dead by the time her brothers and her husband were able to get her to the hospital.*

Even though the newspapers said Katherine drank acid by accident instead of pain medication, her daughter, who was nine at the time, gave a very different version of events. She remembers her mother and uncles arguing about who was responsible for Mamie's death. Katherine yelled something about losing faith in her brothers. In an angry fit, she ran upstairs, grabbed the poison and drank it in front of them in a suicidal act of defiance.

Death kept circling the Fees, and ten years later, in 1935, Frank's son died in a strange airplane accident. He was a colonel in the army, and the plane he was on hit a radio guywire and crashed near Dallas, Texas. The son had sold the Fee house two years before his death.

After the Fees owned the home, the house didn't see as much tragedy. In 1943, a tenant in the home fell down the stairs. And then the home went through a few hands. The house was sectioned off and turned into an apartment building. Then it was abandoned and closed off for over twenty years.

The new owners bought it in 2019 and have been renovating it, trying to bring it back to its old splendor. They currently host paranormal investigations in the building. To book the home for an investigation, reach out to Drew on the Fee House Facebook page.

Some of the phenomena in the house include a strong male presence, weird feelings around the stairs, faces in the windows and clear EVPs that say, "Welcome."

THE AUTHOR'S EXPERIENCES AT THE FEE HOUSE

The Fee House is one of the strangest places I have ever investigated. It's not the most haunted, but it's got a strange energy that permeates the place that I haven't felt anywhere else.

I dreamed about the Fee House before I ever saw it. It's strange how I even ended up there in the first place. There were a series of events that happened at the Crescent Hotel in Eureka Springs that brought me to an investigation at the Fee House. Those events were predicted by a spirit box and a Ouija board. My friend Stephanie and I were told to go downstairs, one floor below us—literally down, underneath us. So, we went one floor down but in the same spot where we were sitting and playing with the talking board.

On a whim, we listened to what the board said and went downstairs. It just so happens that one of the most haunted parts of the hotel was directly below us. There, we met another investigator, who invited us to the Fee House. Stephanie lived in another state at the time. I lived only three hours away, so I took a leap of faith and went to the investigation.

There was exactly one week between the time I investigated the Crescent Hotel and the Fee House. About three days before I traveled to Little Rock, I had a strange dream about being in the dining room of the Fee House. I remember there being a table in the middle of the room and chairs. I remember seeing a fireplace in an adjoining room. In the middle of the table, there was a portal. There were spirits going in and out of the portal and looking around the place. Out of nowhere, a woman showed up. I am not sure if she came from the portal or if she was already in the house.

She had dark hair and dark eyes. She looked frail and she was wearing a bright blue '50s Jackie Onassis–type Chanel suit, complete with a pillbox hat. There was something off about her, and I couldn't place it. She seemed to be in the wrong period, or she appeared this way on purpose. The woman walked up to me and started screaming. She screamed so loudly that it woke me up. Needless to say, I was a little bit hesitant to go to the Fee House after the dream. It's not usual for me to dream about places before I go to them, and I figured whoever this blue lady was, she wanted to talk and have her story told.

Both times I've investigated at the Fee House, it's been undergoing renovations. There were no working bathrooms, no running water and only one set of electrical sockets that worked in one room, which was the office of the owner. During the investigation, an extension cord ran from the office to the dining room as a solitary source of light.

The dining room ended up being the meet-up place because of the big wooden table in the middle of the room and the chairs—also because it had the only electrical outlet where cellphones and equipment could be charged up. It was a slow process, but it was better than nothing.

I was surprised that the table and the dining room looked a lot like what I saw in my dream. I didn't recognize any other parts of the house. It was interesting that the table was where everyone came and went. I'm not sure if it had a portal, but the energy in that room was completely different from the energy in the rest of the house.

The second time I went to the Fee House, Stephanie and my friend Buck went with me. Stephanie and I made sure to bring our dowsing rods to find out if and why the dining room had such a weird energy. We realized that the energy was like a column that moved up the dining room, into the other floors of the house and straight up into the attic. So, if there was a portal, it would affect all floors in the house, especially in that area.

When we went up the stairs and into the more haunted areas of the house, we realized they were all stacked on top of each other. It was like a column of energy that might be considered a portal. Maybe it was more like a concentrated pooling of energy that fostered paranormal activity.

Stephanie and I were curious why the energy was pooled in that specific area. So, we pulled out our dowsing rods to see if there were any ley lines or energy fields that could affect the environment. We went outside, and through some dowsing, we realized there were two major lines of energy called dragon lines that intersected directly in the middle of the dining room. This crossing of energy would definitely create a large pool of magnetic energy that would theoretically feed paranormal activity, especially if there were all kinds of high-energy experiences that heightened the energy.

The Fees were definitely a family with all kinds of secrets. Their friends fed off of the gossip that circled around them. I'm sure some of it was hearsay, but most gossip is based in some kind of truth. Through my research, I've found that both Mamie and Frank may have been sleeping with the help. And there may have been ongoing dissention between the siblings.

This would make sense as to why Katherine ran upstairs, took the acid and killed herself in front of her brothers. I can only go off stories I've been told and my own psychic investigating at the Fee House. However, there does seem to be an overarching issue between Katherine and her brothers. Some kind of secret that they carried. It could be something innocuous that got out of hand over time because it was never resolved, or it could be something of a scandalous nature.

From the investigation I did with Stephanie and Buck, we feel there was definitely something going on. The brothers and Katherine weren't just fighting over Mamie's death. There was something else going on, and she was tired. She was tired of the lies, and she was tired of being a pawn. She was overemotional and did something that she knew would scare them for life. It was her big F-you to her family. I will never believe that Katherine's death was an accident.

There is a picture of Katherine in the Fee House, and I've been told that she was a little off. Family members have said she was emotional and could be hysterical. Somebody told me that she had "crazy eyes," like she wasn't all there. So, perhaps she had a mental illness that was left unchecked and moved into histrionics when she couldn't regulate her emotions. Again, this is all conjecture and what we felt from our investigating. The only people who know what really happened are all dead.

The first time I investigated the Fee House, I had that dream still in my head and wondered who the "blue lady" was and why she was screaming at me. After doing some research and getting more information about the deaths that occurred in the house, I think the screaming lady was Mamie.

On the second floor is Mamie's room. The fireplace where she accidentally set herself on fire is still there in the room. It's a very active place in the house. K2 meters go off in that room, even though there is no electricity anywhere on the second floor.

You can put a motion detector or a rem pod near the fireplace, and they will get triggered, even though no one is sitting anywhere near the equipment. In Mamie's room, you can get really clear EVPs, and she will communicate through spirit boxes very clearly.

When Mamie accidentally set herself on fire, she was said to be wearing a blue dress. The bricks edging the fireplace are also light blue. The woman in my dream was wearing a blue suit. It was definitely the wrong era, but she did have the energy of a matriarch. I never understood why she was screaming. The only thing that comes to mind is that there were a lot of secrets in the house, and nobody was listening. Everyone took their secrets to their graves, including Katherine. It seems Katherine is the only one who tried to say something or get the words out. Instead of telling the truth, she decided to get even and kill herself instead.

I believe that Frank haunts the house, even though he died somewhere else. There have been many reports of a man looking out the attic window. Sometimes, people see someone on the second floor. Every time I've gone to the house, I've felt the presence of a tall man wearing some kind of suit. One time, I saw him looking at a pocket watch and pacing in the attic. Other times, I've felt him following me around.

For some reason, both Mamie and Frank seem to be attached to the house. Maybe they were proud of the life they had together in that house, even though it was full of secrets. Or maybe it made them feel special or like they mattered. It could have given them the status they felt they deserved, having servants and living in a prestigious part of town. Or maybe, even after death, they wanted to be close to the place where all their secrets lie. Maybe they are still protecting what they don't want to come out.

What I think is the strangest thing about the Fee House is that there were a lot of years when the house was owned by other people. More years have gone by with other people owning the house than the years the Fees lived there. Yet their energy is the only energy that shows up. It's prominent and doesn't die.

I could feel that something happened on the stairs. I felt someone fall. But then I also felt an argument and yelling. I felt there was some kind of "accident" that wasn't really an accident. This was during my initial walkthrough, when I didn't know the history of the building. So, their energy is the spirit of the place. I don't think they will ever leave. Whatever they are hiding, they have literally taken it to their graves.

The Haunted Holler

Fayetteville

Just outside of Fayetteville, there's a valley the locals call a "holler," where the Confederate Cemetery resides. There's a hill nearby where it is said the Sequoyah tribe created the Cherokee Outlet. It's an area steeped in rich folklore—and ghosts.

Just outside the cemetery grounds, to the east in the holler, there's a popular tale about a screaming specter woman called the burning bride. The story says that in the 1850s, a newlywed couple built a modest log cabin in the valley. On the evening of their wedding day, they went to their new home to start their new life. Outside, they built a fire to do the cooking and to stay warm. The groom went inside to retrieve something while the bride stayed outside and stoked the fire. A burning ember got caught in her skirt and lit her on fire. Panicked, the bride ran into the woods, flailing and screaming, trying to put out the flames encapsulating her clothes—only the fire spread too fast. Her husband realized she was gone and went looking for his bride. He found her burned to a crisp, lying in the dirt of the holler.

Now, the holler is a popular hiking spot. Many have said they've heard a woman screaming in the woods at night, especially on cold fall evenings. Others have witnessed the sight of a phantom fire or the edge light of clothes burning, even though there isn't a person in them.

In the same area, there's another story of a ghostly woman, but this one doesn't have an origin, and some believe it might have been made up to cover up some nefarious shenanigans going in the woods. People in the area talk of hearing the loud clomping of a galloping horse running through the holler. When they search the woods for the horse, they see a woman wearing a white gown with her head missing.

In the 1950s, a woman named Ida Knerr purchased a piece of property in the holler. She believed the story of the headless woman in white was invented by locals who were using the woods for gambling rackets. The urban legend kept people out of the woods for fear they would be chased by a headless woman riding a phantom horse. This kept the gamblers under the radar of the law.

The Author's Experience at the Haunted Holler

The Haunted Holler is located across the street from the Fayetteville Confederate Soldier Cemetery, which is peaceful and well-manicured. Surrounded by a quaint stone wall with an iron gate, the cemetery is tidy and organized with streamlined rows of white headstones commemorating forgotten soldiers.

Across the street, the forest is tangled, wild and haphazard. In the uneven hilly earth, there are the ruins of an old 1800s cemetery with broken headstones strewn about and twisted pieces of wire that used to be the fenced parameter for square family plots. Some headstones lie against trees. Others are missing everything but their bases. Other graves dip like sinkholes because of the erosion from the snow and rain in the area.

If you go farther into the forest, the air smells of burned wood, and you can see the charring on the trees. Some of the branches have fallen onto the ground, and others are bent and lie broken on the ground. The energy of the place hangs heavy, and it hit me in the chest. It felt like I was trying to breathe underwater. I noticed how quiet the woods were without the singing of birds or the rustle of the usual small critters. Usually, the Northwest Ozark woods are full of the scampering noises of fat, bushy squirrels. This area of the woods had an eerie silence that made it unnerving. It's not a peaceful place.

The only energetic reprieve is a stream that goes through the holler. The swollen waterway seemed to break up the negativity and wash it downstream. However, when you cross the stream, the energy gets thick again. I stood in one spot and closed my eyes to take in the energy, hoping I could bypass the eerie feelings and maybe cobble together some pieces of psychic information.

I realized that the heaviness I felt in my chest was from a gunshot wound. There was an altercation in the woods. I saw two men fighting in the woods and a woman pleading for them to stop and put down their guns. From the clothes of the woman, I ascertained this must of have occurred during the 1800s or early 1900s. She wore a thick, dark-colored, long skirt that seemed to be made of a natural material. From the heaviness, I thought it could be wool. Her dark brown hair was pulled up behind her head. The men had on off-white long-sleeve shirts, and one of them wore a short beard. I was seeing the psychic vision from the perspective of the man who got shot. He was drunk. The other man seemed heated, but he must have been inebriated as well. While the woman was screaming, both men pulled out their guns, but the other man drew faster, and I could feel the bullet go through the first man's chest at close range. He fell down and died very quickly. I could hear the woman screaming in my head, and I'm sure that the residual of her voice could probably still be heard in the forest.

I didn't get a sense of a headless woman ghost or a burning woman running through the trees. The burned parts of the trees were definitely modern, and the smell was too fresh to be residual. However, I'm sure there were other things that happened in the forest. Whether it be gambling or lover quarrels or drunken shenanigans, the trees definitely hold the secrets of the past.

The Ozarks are absolutely beautiful. One can't help but be in awe of the vast wilderness and primal energy that inhabits the wild. Some parts have never been inhabited at all, and others are now reclaimed by the wild. East Mountain Cemetery and Monte Ne Resort are some of those places.

THE MANSION AND THE THING IN THE WOODS

After my initial reactions to the haunted hollow, I was told by a local that I was close to the holler but that I didn't go far enough into the forest. The actual location of the hollow was up the road a bit and on private property just past an 1800s mansion that belonged to a heavy-hitting politician in the area.

Of course, I had to check it out to see if this new information was based in any truth. So, I set out one night to see if I could discover this mansion and see how far away it was from the location I originally thought was the hollow. I went to the East Mountain Cemetery and then realized there is another road to the right that goes straight into the woods. It has a sign that reads "Dead End," so I assumed that it was someone's driveway and didn't think much about it the first time I was in the area. However, this time, I went up the road to see what was up there, and it did not disappoint.

The paved road went up on an incline and then evened out. The trees hung over the road and connected, turning it into what seemed like a tunnel. After about a quarter of a mile, the tunnel opened up. On the lefthand side, there stood an 1800s-style two-story mansion. In the middle of the night, the giant house looked abandoned and dilapidated. The lights were off, and it looked like there was all kinds of stuff stored on the lawn and near the front door. I wanted to get out of the car and peek around, but honestly, the area was a little bit spooky that night. A heaviness lingered in the air, and I felt like someone or something was watching me from the woods. It made the hair on my arms stand up, and I felt uneasy. Even though I was more curious than scared, I decided it was better to leave the thing in the woods alone and come back another time during the day to stake out the area.

Two weeks later, I went back to do some more recon and to see if I could figure out what was going on with that mansion. This time, I didn't drive my car. Instead, I walked up the dead-end road with my friend Kelli and one other person. The feeling of being watched wasn't as strong this time, except in one area that had the remnants of a brick retaining wall. The heaviness was still there, only this time, it came with a sense of dizziness. We surmised that maybe something significant had happened in the area. There were bricks that looked like they had been burned by fire. Maybe there had been some truth to the legend about the woman running through the forest and accidentally killing herself. Maybe the house had burned down, too. Maybe it created some kind of thinning in the ether, which created a vortex or a portal.

I used my dowsing rods to see if I could gauge a difference in the energy of that specific area. I followed the rods until they took me to an area about five hundred yards from the broken-down brick retaining wall. It had a pile of bricks that looked like it was part of a structure that had fallen in on itself. It didn't look like a house foundation. We questioned if it was a well or similar kind of structure and if the dowsing rods were picking up on the water that probably still pooled underground. It definitely had a weird, dizzying energy, much like the brick wall.

We tried to use the spirit box to talk to whatever was in the woods to see if we could get any information. The box talked about Native ancestors and more than one spirit. It alluded that the thing in the woods that watched us was more than one energy. It was a conglomeration of ancient ancestors, forest elementals and something much older that didn't want to be forgotten. They were coming near us because we were paying attention.

This area of the woods was just short of the where the mansion was located. Our group decided to keep going, get out of the woods and walk up the street to get a peek of the house. Maybe we could figure out the alleged true location of the haunted hollow. In another five minutes, we were face to face with the 1800s southern-style house surrounded by a modern-looking fence. Behind the fence were four dogs running toward us, barking at full volume. It was a confusing sight. The house seemed run down, and the stuff I thought I saw at night were kids' toys and some kind of colorful plastic playground. It seemed odd against the background of this larger-than-life historical landmark. There were things near the front door, and the whole place looked a little cluttered and messy. We stood for a couple of minutes, taking in the scene. Then we saw an older woman walk from the backyard. She stayed far away but was definitely checking us out. We waved and smiled but turned around and walked back down the road, not wanting to intrude on her property.

We never figured out what was going on with the retaining wall and the weird pile of bricks. I did some research on the internet when I got home, but there was no mention of what was on the property. We did find some information about the mansion, its connection to the cemetery and the haunted holler. It all goes together.

After our adventure with the weirdness in the woods and the mansion, we decided to take a break and sit in the gazebo at the Confederate cemetery. One of my friends knows the caretaker of the cemetery, who lives on the premises. He just happened to see the caretaker walking by and waved him down. My friend asked the caretaker to give us some history of the cemeteries and the area to hopefully fill in some gaps. This is how we figured out how everything went together.

The caretaker went on to tell us about the Walker family. David Walker was a lawyer and political activist who became a judge in the 1800s. He had a lot of influence during the Civil War and was related to George Washington by marriage. His family plot, which includes some of the Washingtons, is located at the hub of the East Mountain Cemetery.

Walker had the two-story mansion up the hill built in 1878 in an Italian style, which was very popular for the time. The front portion of the house was built in 1872 by another person named Mathew Leeper. Walker built onto the other house, making it what is today. His daughter lived in the house with her husband until their deaths. The house is just over three thousand square feet, and it was listed in the National Register of Historic Places in 1975.

The Walkers enslaved people until after the Civil War. It is said there were other settlements around the house, including those belonging to the Walkers' indentured servants. It is unclear if the retaining wall and the other pile of bricks we encountered had anything to do with the Walker house or if it was another housing settlement from someone who had claimed a parcel.

However, East Mountain Cemetery did have enslaved people buried there. It is an assumption that the bodies were those of the people enslaved by the Walker family or other known relatives in the area. No one really knows the truth, however, because the gravestones are not where they should be. I described previously how the headstones were strewn about against trees and piled in places.

It is said the reason the cemetery is in such disrepair—aside from the Walker family plots, which are well taken care of—is because the water company or other utility companies dug up the cemetery when they put in the underground utility lines and basically put the broken or misappropriated headstones in a pile. They figured the cemetery was old and of no consequence and didn't take the time to keep things how they left them.

I could not get proof of this story, so it's just conjecture at this point, but it does feel like something that could have happened. I have heard of things like this happening before in other towns. It's just a basic disrespect for the dead with no regard for sacred ground or ancestral lineage, especially of those of color in an area that largely sided with the Confederacy. Whether this story is true or not, there are a lot of graves that are missing their gravestones, have been buried or are lost to time and the shifting landscape.

In 2014, the University of Arkansas, in conjunction with the Northwest Arkansas African American Heritage Association (NWA-AAHA), bought the land in order to survey the cemetery, find the lost graves and put names to those who have been buried there and forgotten. In January 2022, the groups finally came together and started their efforts. They believe that there are between eighty and one hundred unmarked graves in the area that belong to enslaved people. Their hope is to put headstones in the graves and research the histories of these lost souls to give them back their heritage.

As for the haunted hollow and the story of the woman running through the woods, I'm not even sure where it is. I never really got a good answer to its real location. The caretaker said he has been in the holler, which he said is behind the Walker house on private property. He said it was hard to get to, and he felt something big chasing him out of the woods, something unseen and scary. Looking at Google Maps, there is a clearing behind the house that dips down. The energy the caretaker talked about certainly seems familiar to the feeling of the thing—whatever it was—that was staring at me the night I went to investigate the house. That sense of something big and otherworldly, staring, watching, waiting.

In the written accounts I have in books and on the internet, there is no mention of the Walker mansion or any kind of housing around the hollow. I followed the directions per the articles I found, and it took me past East Mountain Cemetery to the place Kelli and I visited the first time. It wasn't a designated hollow, per se, but it was a clearing that dipped down between two sides of a forest. It did have the feeling of being haunted there. It had that otherworldly energy. However, now that I know the history of the cemetery, it could be that the entire area is haunted by its history.

There are the forgotten souls of the Confederate soldiers across the street. There are just as many blank headstones in that cemetery, even though they weren't enslaved. They were still tossed aside. After the Civil War, no one wanted to deal with the Confederate dead because they were seen as traitors.

At the East Mountain Cemetery, nobody seemed to care about the enslaved servants of the Walker family. Their history and their grave markers were tossed aside and forgotten, because at the time, they weren't considered important. They were little more than property. Then there were the gamblers and sinners drinking and making bets in those trees, making up stories about a headless horsewoman to scare off the locals. If that wasn't weird enough, part of the land was deemed a dumping site for bottles and cans and other trash.

Somewhere in all of this weird history, there is possibly a woman who lost her own life in an accident, a weird snafu in which she caught herself on fire and went running through the woods. This strange story is what brought me to this land. She is an almost forgotten tale. Perhaps her ghost is the gateway to other forgotten stories, and the entire area is a vortex of souls that long to have their stories told. Hopefully, by writing this entry in this book, it sheds light on the area and readers will take the time to visit the area and honor those lost and forgotten. Give them reverence and listen. Maybe they will tell you about their tales through a sighting or an EVP, or maybe they will just be a whisper in the wind.

KELLI'S EXPERIENCE AT THE HAUNTED HOLLER

The land sitting just outside of downtown is its own anomaly. This little patch of wild has somehow managed to remain untouched since 1804. As a sensitive person, I could feel the length of its story and the breadth of the forest as soon as I put the car in the park.

Sitting across a gravel road from the well-maintained Confederate cemetery, the neglect of this historic cemetery was overwhelming. In the Ozarks, families have a tradition of future generations maintaining and caring for family plots. Some cemeteries are loved and maintained, oftentimes on a plot of family land owned and maintained for generations—not here. The decrepit forest and broken marble headstones were the norm for the forgotten stories in the ground here. What was likely a small community's plot for loved ones has been left to the wilds for reclamation. Grave depressions scattered across the northern corner have no headstones, leaving a painful twinge of grief for lifetimes forgotten.

The weeping iron fencing around sectioned family plots carries the weight of sorrow and reverence lost to the years. Families have moved on, and their stories are forgotten, no keepers to maintain their place of rest or tell their stories. This neglect and forgottenness is now the state of this cemetery, with the exception of one headstone.

Simply marked "SALLY," this grave site holds notes of Ozarkian heritage still thriving around her sweet little grave. The top of the headstone is adorned with coins and small rocks, a tradition likely brought over with the migration of European settlers. It was comforting to see some of our old practices have not been forgotten, even if only in this two-by-four-foot section of earth.

The holler itself was reclaimed by the wilds long ago. Very little evidence of human inhabitants can be found outside of half-buried pots and old glass wine pints. Nature has prevailed. I think what makes this place so unique is the overall liminality of the forest itself. In many places of old wood, the elder trees look down in wisdom, watching as each new generation searches again for her secrets. This forest was different. The old trees look down in sadness, mourning their coming passing. Many have already lost their larger limbs or are being suffocated by parasitic vines. The cemetery itself is riddled with fallen trees waiting for removal.

As we ventured farther into the holler, the brush became thicker and increasingly tangled. Polypore conks grew in abundance as a sign of great trees in decomposition. Eventually, we were forced to scramble over the thickets, giving a feel of extra entanglement to the area. The forest is thriving, but the trees are actively dying, untouched by humans and left to their own devices on how to move forward from time passed. New generations of oaks are sprouting up around the dying spirits of the old.

We were in the wilds, not a space for flippant humans, a place of reverence and the ongoing cycle of death and rebirth. This little pocket of great wilds became more evident as we trekked on. Here, we began to experience the magic of the wild. Two separate herds of deer in just a couple acres of wood presented themselves, each group curious but not afraid. They led us across old property lines in the direction of what I can safely assume was once a homestead site or, according to legend, a possible gambling den. The jonquils spoke of past landscaping and, through symbolism, a death giving life to a new beginning.

Curiously, we didn't see any other people the entire time we were there—no cars, no people, just dying things and dying stories. Some of the themes from folklore were there, charred remains of trees past that gave a hint of fire in the past now bringing nourishment and life to the thick brush that inhabits the area. This just another sign of the sacred process of death and rebirth.

Just like many things in life, our figurative deaths bring change and transformation. This new life is only able to spring forth in a space of breaking down, an energy of decay and laying to rest. Oftentimes, we must lay things down forever and let them be forgotten so that we may make space for a new generation or new life to emerge. However, just like this cemetery, if these things are not revered and honored, in their passing, they can leave a lingering feeling of neglect and disregard that is waiting to be healed. Thanks to the city of Fayetteville, East Mountain Cemetery will get a facelift and, hopefully, a new generation of reverence and appreciation of the things that came before us.

For now, this land sits in decay, waiting for its time of renewal or maybe just maintaining its wilderness. If there's anything I've learned in my time in the Natural State, it's how powerful the wild can be and how much we only think we own. Some places aren't meant to be tamed, and almost all places require the passing of time and decay to spring forth as something new.

The lessons of the ever-present cycle of death and rebirth are alive and well within the forests around us. One must only hold reverence for this sacred cycle and be open to seeing the blessings it holds.

Confederate Cemetery

Fayetteville

514 East Rock Street
Fayetteville, AR 72701

The Confederate Cemetery was created for the confederate soldiers from the Battle of Prairie Grove, the Battle of Pea Ridge and other skirmishes, like the Battle of Fayetteville. Some died from illness and disease in the camps, while others died in battle and then were dumped like trash in side-of-the-road graves.

Since the Union won the Civil War, the United States government already had a plan for the soldiers who fought on their side. Arkansas had an official veterans' national cemetery commissioned in Fayetteville shortly after the war had ended. The dead were accounted for, and their families were contacted. They were very much treated like heroes.

On the other side, the Confederate soldiers were seen as traitors. Their bodies were collected and dumped. None of their names were researched or their families contacted. They were not considered veterans and never treated as such.

People, especially those in the South, wanted their dead. The families of the missing soldiers wanted to know where their relatives were. They thought the dead deserved some kind of real burial. A committee was put together, and an article in the newspaper requested volunteers who would help put together an association to deal with the soldiers of the Confederacy. They called themselves the Southern Memorial Association.

The organization started raising funds in 1872. The group bought 3.48 acres of land from Walkers for $150 right across the street from the family's family plot. In March 1873, the Southern Memorial Association contracted J.D. Henry to start looking for Confederate bodies at the state's two largest battle sites. For the Pea Ridge Battlefield, a $1.40 reward was given for each body retrieved. For the Prairie Grove Battlefield, $2.50 was given for each soldier's body.

In the first year, the association collected about three hundred bodies. It cost around $1,200 to build the fence, clean the land and rebury of all the Confederates. The money was raised by hosting fundraising dinners, theatrical performances and bazaars. Throughout the years, the cemetery brought in about five hundred soldiers, which made up about eight hundred total.

The cemetery was quartered by state: one each for Arkansas, Texas, Missouri and Louisiana. As the funds came, additions were made to the cemetery. A simple wood fence was put up around the cemetery, and then it was replaced in 1885. In 1876, the graves were adorned with sandstone headstones and foot markers. They were upgraded to marble in 1903. A cut stone wall was added in 1926–27 for $682.

In 1896, the association decided it wanted to have a monument erected in the middle of the cemetery. Fundraising started specifically for the art installation; it included recitals, card and Parcheesi tournaments and song contests. By 1897, the group had raised approximately $2,000 of the $2,500 needed. Sixteen monument designs were submitted, and the F.H. Venn Company of Memphis, Tennessee, won the bid. On June 10, 1897, the monument had a dedication ceremony that included a float of women from the southern states, university cadets, a group of veterans followed by the drum corps and a carriage that carried the women of the Southern Memorial Association. Some fraternities came to commemorate the memorial, including the Oddfellows and the Knights of Pythias from Missouri.

THE GHOSTS OF THE CONFEDERACY

The Confederate Cemetery is another intersection for the forgotten. No matter your political beliefs, the men who fought in the Civil War still had families. Most were very young and thought they were doing the right thing. At the end of the day, they are still a part of humanity, even though they were treated like they didn't matter.

It's not a coincidence that the Confederate Cemetery is right across the street from the East Mountain Cemetery, where the Walker family sits in a nicely gated plot with large, chiseled marble grave markers.

Around the Walkers are broken gravestones. Some are in piles. Others sit against trees. Some are buried a few inches deep under soil that has been moved from rain and time. The graves belonged to the enslaved, the folks in town who were considered little more than property. They didn't matter, and for all intents and purposes, history would like to erase them and pretend they never existed.

It's funny how the Confederates and the enslaved had a lot in common. They were basically dumped in the same area and given a little bit of space to call their own. Just like with the East Mountain Cemetery, most of the headstones in the Confederate Cemetery don't have names. They don't have a history or a legacy to call their own. They are left behind because of who they were and what they believed in. The enslaved didn't have a choice on what to believe. They were definitely extensions of their owners. However, they too do not have a legacy or a lineage. They don't have a story that can ever be told, because no one knows they even existed.

I have heard stories about the Confederate Cemetery ghosts. Most are innocuous and wandering, like they have no purpose. The caretaker of the cemetery told a story about seeing a man in a Confederate uniform sitting on one of the headstones. He was quiet and contemplative, so the groundskeeper didn't think much of it until he realized that the uniform was from the 1800s. Once his brain caught up, he turned to look at the soldier again, but he was gone.

Others have also seen Confederate soldiers walking around wandering the cemetery. Another common phenomenon is hearing disembodied voices in the cemetery when no one is there. It's like the ghosts of the dead are talking among themselves, since no one else remembers them.

The Author's Experiences
at the Confederate Cemetery

I've been to the cemetery a few times. I have had experiences during the day and in the dark of night. The paranormal phenomenon happens when it wants to, and there's no rhyme or reason for it.

Despite the paranormal undertones, the Confederate Cemetery has a serene energy. It's nestled on a street above downtown Fayetteville, but you would never know because of how remote it feels. The East Mountain Cemetery across the street is in a forest clearing. There are houses all around, but there is very little traffic. I've been there for hours and have not seen a single car or person show up. Even if you drive a quarter mile, you would be on one of the main streets in Fayetteville. It almost gives you the feeling of being lost in time.

On my first visit to the cemetery, I went with my friend Kelli and my mom. It was an interesting, solemn experience, mostly because we realized there were hundreds of dead buried there, and most of the gravestones were blank. It was then that we realized these men were tossed aside by their own country. They, in essence, had no home. If history had been different and the Confederacy had won, these same men would have been heroes. Their families would have been honored and commemorated for their service.

The second time I went to the cemetery, I went for a paranormal investigation to see if I could experience any of the phenomenon. I went at night and took a male friend just to be safe. It was a completely different experience—not as serene or calm. The dead wanted to talk and made sure I knew about it.

One of the first things I experienced was like nothing I'd seen before, and it happened with my spirit box. I have used my box a lot over the years. So, I am really aware of how it works and what it does. This night, the spirit box did something really weird.

On the front of the ITC device, there's a small button that turns the radio from AM to FM. If you push it long enough, a red light comes on for temperature. I have hit the button sometimes and accidentally turned on the temperature reading. It makes a beeping noise but then it stops. All you have to do is hit the button again, and it goes back to AM or FM.

On this night, the box decided to malfunction and stay in temperature mode. I kept hitting the button, and it wouldn't go back to the AM and FM function. Instead, it started to beep loudly over and over again in a pattern. After I got over the initial freak-out, my friend and I realized that the beeping sounded like Morse code or something similar. Unfortunately, I don't know Morse code. My friend didn't either.

We listened to it for a while, trying to figure out what it meant. I kept trying to push the button to get it to stop, and it finally did. It didn't happen for the rest of the night. Looking at a Morse code table, I deciphered that what I heard either created a "J" or an "I"—and that's only if I remembered it correctly.

The letter "J" would make sense, because in a later spirit box session, we got the name John more than once. In fact, in every spirit box session I've done at the cemetery, the name John comes through. I still haven't figured out who he is. For all intents and purposes, he could be one of the forgotten soldiers trying to come through and let us know he's there. Maybe he wanted to tell his story.

During the rest of the spirit box session, we had some interesting things come through. One of the most meaningful to me was the phrase "We are Americans."

To me and my friend, it meant that these soldiers on this hill, all but forgotten, want us to know they are still part of our history. They still feel like they belong, and they don't understand why they were treated so badly. They want to tell their story. We told them we understood, and we considered them to be American, despite their beliefs or what side they fought on. It was a strange, bittersweet moment.

Another weird thing happened that night. I saw a Confederate soldier out of the corner of my eye. I was sitting in my car on the driver's side. The soldier walked past my window and then to the back of the car and disappeared. I thought I was imagining things, because I turned and barely got a glimpse.

The only thing that made me believe what I saw were my friend's words, "Did you see him?" I answered yes. My friend said he saw a soldier walk from the cemetery, to the side of my car and then disappear as he passed by the back window. I wonder if it was someone who had talked on the spirit box and wanted us to know that he was a real person.

The last thing that happened to me occurred on a different day. I had gone to the cemetery a third time with my friend Buck to take pictures for this book. He was twenty minutes behind me. So, I got out of the car to look around. First, I went over to the Walker family plot, because some things had changed. The University of Arizona had obviously been out to the cemetery and surveyed some new grave areas.

After I looked around, I walked toward the Confederate Cemetery. Out of nowhere, I heard voices. It was if I was overhearing a conversation with a group of men. I looked around and realized there was only one car parked next to mine. I went through the cemetery gate to look around and find out where the conversation had come from. The only person I saw was a man walking his dog. The dog and the man were quiet to the point that I had no idea they were even there. It made me a little suspicious that they might not even exist, so I watched the man walk with his dog to his car and drive away, just to make sure he was in this reality.

Maybe I misinterpreted the man talking to his dog? Maybe he sounded like more than one voice? I'm not sure. I could swear that I heard more than one voice, like a group of men quietly talking, almost like they were in a huddle. I know there weren't any other people around. During the next fifteen or so minutes, it was eerily quiet. There were no birds chirping and no other sounds. I didn't pull out any of my equipment, because my friend Buck showed up, and we went straight to business.

If you get a chance to go to the Confederate Cemetery and walk around, tell "John" I sent you. Or if you decide to do some investigating of your own, know that the dead there want to tell their tales. All you have to do is listen.

Prairie Grove Battlefield State Park

506 East Douglas Street
Prairie Grove, AR 72753

The Battle of Prairie Grove was fought on December 7, 1862, in Northwest Arkansas, and it was one of the largest Civil War battles fought west of the Mississippi River. The Confederate army, under the command of General Thomas Hindman, sought to drive the Union forces out of Northwest Arkansas and regain control of the state. Meanwhile, the Union army, under the command of General James G. Blunt, was determined to prevent the Confederates from gaining the upper hand in the region. The battle was fought over a four-mile area and lasted for almost twelve hours. It was a critical battle fought over the control of Northwest Arkansas and for the strategic initiative in the region.

As the sun rose on the morning of December 7, both armies made their final preparations for battle. The Union forces under Blunt were positioned along the east–west Telegraph Road, with the artillery placed on a high ridge to the north. Meanwhile, the Confederate forces under Hindman were positioned in a defensive line just south of the road, with their artillery on a hill to the south.

The Confederates initially had the upper hand, but the Union army was able to push them back and eventually secured the field. General Blunt was instrumental in the Union victory, as he led a daring counterattack that turned the tide of the battle in favor of the Union army. One of the most notable aspects of the Battle of Prairie Grove was the fighting that occurred near the Borden house. The house, which was owned by a Confederate sympathizer, was used by the Confederates as a hospital during the battle. The fighting around the house was some of the most intense of the entire battle, as both sides fought fiercely for control of the area.

At one point during the battle, the Confederates set fire to the house, forcing the wounded and dying Union soldiers inside to either burn or try to escape the flames. The scene was a horrific one, as the screams of the wounded soldiers could be heard for miles around. Despite the tragedy, the Union army was able to hold its ground and eventually push the Confederates back. After the battle, both sides claimed victory, but it was clear the Union forces had achieved their objective of preventing the Confederate forces from reaching Missouri.

Blunt, seeing that the Confederate forces were beginning to waver, ordered a counterattack against the Confederate left flank. This attack was led by Colonel James M. Williams, who had been leading a successful guerrilla campaign against Confederate forces in Missouri prior to the battle. Williams and his men charged down the hill toward the Confederate lines, causing panic and confusion among the Confederate soldiers. The Union counterattack was successful, and the Confederate forces began to retreat. However, Hindman rallied his troops and launched a final attack against the Union forces. The fighting was fierce, with hand-to-hand combat occurring in some places.

In the end, the Union forces held their ground, and the Confederate forces were forced to retreat. The Battle of Prairie Grove was over. The casualty figures for the battle are unclear, but it is estimated that the Union forces suffered around 1,200 casualties, while the Confederate forces suffered around 2,700. Despite their numerical superiority, the Confederate forces were unable to achieve victory at Prairie Grove, due in part to the skill and determination of the Union troops but also due to strategic mistakes made by Hindman.

General James G. Blunt, who led the Union army to victory at the Battle of Prairie Grove, was one of the most important figures in the conflict in Northwest Arkansas. Blunt was a seasoned veteran of the Indian Wars and had extensive experience in fighting Native tribes on the western frontier. He was known for his aggressive tactics and willingness to take risks in battle. Blunt demonstrated his leadership skills and tactical acumen by leading a daring counterattack that turned the tide of the war.

Blunt's victory at the Battle of Prairie Grove was a significant turning point in the Civil War in the trans-Mississippi theater. The Union forces were able to prevent the Confederates from gaining control of Northwest Arkansas and Missouri, and the Union army was able to secure its hold on the region.

Blunt's success at Prairie Grove also paved the way for future Union victories in the region. With the Confederates on the defensive, the Union army was able to launch a series of successful campaigns in Arkansas, Missouri and Louisiana, which eventually led to the defeat of the Confederacy in the West.

Today, the Battle of Prairie Grove is remembered as one of the most significant engagements of the Civil War in the trans-Mississippi theater. The battlefield is preserved as Prairie Grove Battlefield State Park, which serves as a testament to the bravery and sacrifice of those who fought there. Visitors to the park can explore the battlefield, tour historic structures and learn more about this important chapter in American history.

Some of the paranormal activity at the state park include war sounds on the battlefield and voices talking. Lights shine through the windows in the Borden house, even though nobody is around. Investigators have gotten crystal-clear EVPs of soldiers talking about the war.

THE AUTHOR'S EXPERIENCE AT THE PRAIRIE GROVE BATTLEFIELD STATE PARK

My friends Kelli and Buck went with me to the Prairie Grove Battlefield State Park. We were curious about the history of the Prairie Grove Battle, so the first thing we did was take the self-guided tour in the museum and watch all of the videos. I had lived in Arkansas for a few years at this point, and I didn't realize how integral the state of Arkansas was to the Union winning the Civil War. Paranormal strangeness aside, it's worth the trip to Prairie Grove, just to witness a small slice of American history.

The battlefield area is much larger than I expected. I normally go into these paranormal adventures without knowing too much about history. In this case, we went in knowing a lot. I had read a little bit about the Borden house and knew that the area around it seemed to have the most paranormal activity, since it encompassed the bloodiest parts of the battle.

The house is a good distance from the museum. So, we got into a car and drove onto the battlefield. The state park has a self-guided driving tour that goes through the entire park. We followed the signs to the Borden house and went to check it out. The energy is definitely different in that part of the field. The only way I can describe it is heavy. It's a little hard to breathe there.

We decided to set up some paranormal equipment on the grass right next to the Borden house to see what would happen. Kelli and I asked questions with the spirit box and did some Estes sessions. Our findings were strange. It was like more than one person was talking, and they were hurried. The voices in the spirit box were talking about the war and being exhausted. They talked about fires and blasts. The answers were short, staccato and rushed. It almost felt like we had gone back in time and were getting a summary of what was happening on the battlefield. The K2 meter went off a few times when we asked if anyone wanted to speak.

I truly feel the soldiers on the Prairie Grove Battlefield want to talk. I feel like they are stuck there because of the cold, the loudness of cannons and the shock of people falling over dead everywhere. I don't think the soldiers knew what they were up against, and those memories will forever stay on the battlefield, haunting anyone who dares to ask the right questions.

PART IV

CREEPY CRYPTIDS

THE BOGGY CREEK MONSTER

FOUKE

In the early 1970s, the small town of Fouke, Arkansas, became the center of a legend of a terrifying creature that was said to be a large, hairy beast that roamed the woods around the town and had been spotted by numerous locals over the years. The sightings were so frequent and widespread that they even inspired a movie, *The Legend of Boggy Creek*, which was released in 1972.

According to reports, the Fouke Monster stands at around seven feet tall and has a powerful, musky odor. Its appearance has been described as being similar to that of a Bigfoot or Sasquatch. It has long arms and shaggy fur covering its body. Some reports claim that the creature has glowing eyes, while others say it makes eerie, howling noises.

The first reported sighting of the Fouke Monster took place in 1971, when a family living in a remote farmhouse just outside of Fouke claimed they encountered the creature. The Ford family reported that they had heard strange noises outside their home late at night and seen a large, hairy creature lurking in the shadows. The creature had apparently torn apart the family's screen door and left claw marks on the walls of their home.

After the Fords' story was published in the local newspaper, other residents of Fouke began coming forward with their own accounts of the Fouke Monster. Some claimed they saw the creature while driving on the roads around the town, while others reported they heard its eerie howls late at night.

As the legend of the Fouke Monster grew, so did the interest in the town itself. Tourists began flocking to Fouke in search of their own encounters with the creature, and many locals started selling souvenirs and merchandise related to the legend. The town even began hosting an annual Fouke Monster Festival, complete with music, food and vendors.

However, not everyone believes in the existence of the Fouke Monster. Skeptics have pointed out that the creature's sightings always seemed to coincide with the release of movies or TV shows about Bigfoot or similar cryptids. Others argue that the sightings are simply the result of misidentifications of other animals, like bears. Some have even claimed they're outright hoaxes.

Despite the skepticism, the legend of the Fouke Monster persists. Even today, there are still reports of sightings of the creature in and around the town of Fouke. Some locals claim that they have heard its eerie howls late at night, while others swear that they have seen the creature lurking in the woods.

So, what is the truth behind the legend of the Fouke Monster? It's impossible to say for sure. Some believe that it's simply a myth, a product of the town's folklore and the imaginations of its residents. Others, however, remain convinced that the creature is real and continue to search for evidence of its existence.

Regardless of whether the Fouke Monster is real or not, its story has become a part of the town of Fouke's history and culture. The legend has inspired books, movies and TV shows, and it continues to draw tourists to the town. Whether you're a believer or a skeptic, the legend of the Fouke Monster is certainly one that will keep you wandering through the woods, wondering if you can catch a glimpse of the creature's furry coat.

THE WHITE RIVER MONSTER

NEWPORT

In the early twentieth century, there were reports of a strange creature lurking in the White River near Newport, Arkansas. The sea creature was dubbed the White River Monster and has been described as being thirty to forty feet long, with gray skin and a spiny ridge along its back. It has often been described as resembling a dinosaur or prehistoric reptile.

The first reported sighting of the White River Monster occurred in 1915, when a local fisherman claimed they saw the creature in the river. Over the years, there were several other sightings and encounters with the creature,

including reports of it attacking boats and making loud roaring noises.

In 1971, two eyewitnesses claimed they encountered the White River Monster while fishing. They described the sea monster as being about twenty feet long, with gray skin and a spiny ridge down its back. They claimed that the monster circled their boat several times before disappearing back into the river.

The White River Monster gained national attention in 1973, when it was reported that several people had seen the creature swimming in the river. The sightings were investigated by a team of researchers from the Smithsonian Institution, who found no evidence of the monster's existence.

Despite the lack of evidence, the legend of the White River Monster lives on in Newport. The creature has become a popular tourist attraction, and there are even festivals held in its honor. In 2017, a statue of the monster was erected in the city.

The Gowrow Monster

Harrison

The Gowrow Monster, also known as the Harrison Monster, is a legendary creature said to inhabit the hills around Harrison, Arkansas. It has been reported to be a large, hairy creature with a human-like face and piercing red eyes. The first reported sighting of the monster occurred in 1971 and was reported by a group of hunters. They claimed they encountered a creature that was over seven feet tall, covered in hair and had glowing red eyes.

Since then, there have been numerous reports of sightings and encounters with the Gowrow Monster. Some locals believe that the monster is a type of Bigfoot or Sasquatch, while others speculate that it could be an unknown species of primate. Despite the numerous sightings, there has never been any concrete evidence of the monster's existence.

The legend of the Gowrow Monster has become a part of Harrison's folklore and has even inspired local businesses and events. In 2013, a local brewery named its American brown ale after the monster, and in 2018, the Harrison Convention and Visitors Bureau held a MonsterFest event, which featured live music, food and a costume contest.

PART V

MURDER AND MAYHEM

THE WEST MEMPHIS THREE

WEST MEMPHIS

The West Memphis Three were three teenagers from West Memphis, Arkansas, who were wrongfully accused of killing three boys in an alleged and completely unsubstantiated ritual.

On May 5, 1993, Michael Moore, Steve Branch and Christopher Byers were reported missing around 7:00 p.m. by John Mark Byers, the adoptive father of one of the children. After 8:00 p.m., the police, neighbors and a search and rescue team canvassed the area, focusing on the Robin Hood Hills area, where the kids were last seen.

The next day, around 1:45 p.m., Parole Officer Steve Jones spotted a black shoe floating in a muddy creek in Robin Hood Hills. With another search, they found the three boys' bodies, naked and hogtied with their own shoelaces. Their clothes were twisted around branches stuck in the creek. Two pairs of underwear were never found.

Initially, police suspected the boys had been beaten on-site and then sexually assaulted. This was due to lacerations found on Christopher Byers's body and the mutilation of his scrotum and penis. The other two boys didn't have any wounds on their nether regions. According to the forensics report, Moore and Branch had died of drowning and multiple injuries, while Byers had died of multiple injuries.

THE THREE VICTIMS

All three boys were eight-year-old second graders at Weaver Elementary School. They were wolves in the Cub Scouts, lived within blocks of each other and were best friends. They were known to always be together and regularly rode their bikes throughout the neighborhood. In 1994, a memorial was erected at the Weaver Elementary playground to honor the three boys. On the twentieth anniversary of the murders, funds were raised to refurbish the memorial.

James Michael Moore

James Michael Moore was considered the leader of the ragtag brood. He had brown hair, stood at four feet, five inches, tall and weighed fifty-five pounds. Moore loved to wear his Boy Scout uniform, even when he wasn't going to meetings. He lived with his parents, Todd and Dana Moore, and his nine-year-old sister. The second grader was last seen wearing blue pants, his Boy Scout uniform shirt and a Boy Scout hat. He was riding his green bike.

Steve Edward Branch

Steve Edward Branch was an honor student at Weaver Elementary School. His mother, Pamela, divorced his biological father when he was an infant. Later, she married Terry Hobbs, his stepfather and one of the last people to see Steve and the boys before they disappeared. The second grader had blond hair, stood four feet, two inches, tall and weighed sixty-four pounds. He was last seen wearing a white T-shirt and blue jeans riding a black and white bicycle.

Christopher Michael Byers

According to his mother, Christopher Michael Byers was a normal little kid who still believed in Santa Claus and the Easter Bunny. His parents divorced when he was four. Shortly afterward, his mother, Melissa, married John Mark Byers, who adopted the boy. Byers had light brown hair, stood four feet tall and weighed fifty-five pounds. He was last seen wearing a white long-sleeved shirt, blue jeans and dark shoes. He wasn't riding his bike the day he disappeared.

The West Memphis Three Suspects

Damien Echols

Considered a cult leader and overseer of the murders, Damien Echols was eighteen years old and a self-proclaimed Wiccan. He had regular run-ins with law enforcement, including previous arrests for vandalism, burglary and shoplifting. His probation officer, Jerry Driver, believed there was a satanic cult in the area. Due to Echols's dark clothes, his heavy metal music tastes and his interest in the occult, Driver was convinced the teenager had founded the cult and was secretly running it behind closed doors. Echols lived with his parents at the Broadway Trailer Park. He had poor grades and barely made it through school. So, he decided to drop out. The teenager served a stint in a mental institution and had issues with grandiosity, hallucinations, depression and mood swings. He had a girlfriend who was pregnant, and he worked part time for a roofing company. Echols frequently hung out with his best friend, Jason Baldwin. They listened to Metallica, read and discussed Stephen King novels, talked to girls on the phone and played video games.

Jason Baldwin

Unlike his best friend, sixteen-year-old Jason Baldwin did well in high school and had a natural talent for drawing and art. He was encouraged to study graphic design in college. Baldwin had some history with law enforcement, mostly getting in trouble with Echols for vandalism and shoplifting. The teenager lived at home with his parents in the Lakeshore neighborhood.

Jessie Misskelley Jr.

Seventeen-year-old Jessie Misskelley Jr. had a low IQ and a bad temper. He was a terrible student and was known to have a short fuse. Misskelley didn't hang out with Echols and Baldwin, but they knew of each other. The teenager had a reputation for starting fights and eventually dropped out of high school. Misskelley lived with his parents at the Highland Trailer Park.

THE 1990s CLIMATE AND SATANIC PANIC

The Satanic Panic phenomenon started in the early 1980s and consisted of the investigation of over twelve thousand cases of unsubstantiated satanic ritual abuse. It stemmed from an overzealous societal fear of the occult, which assumed that any kind of practice outside of Christianity had satanic roots. The devil seemed to have his hand in everything in the 1980s—from *Dungeons and Dragons* and heavy metal music to local daycare centers, nothing seemed safe from demonic forces.

Media outlets fueled the mass hysteria with exclusive specials on the fast-spreading occult frenzy that seemed to grip the United States and then the rest of the world. In 1998, Geraldo Rivera produced a documentary called *Devil Worship: Exposing Satan's Underground.* In the special, he investigated occult-related crimes and dark satanic music and then spoke with self-proclaimed satanists. The two-hour documentary aired on a Tuesday and took over the ratings. Almost twenty million households tuned in to get the official word on how satanic cult practices quietly but surreptitiously infected the minds of children.

It made the devil tangible. He was no longer secluded to the fiery flames of the Underworld. Instead, he was infecting the minds of the neighbors next door. Anyone could be a child-killing satanist and you wouldn't even know it. This narrative started in 1980 with the publication of, according to Wikipedia, a "memoir, *Michelle Remembers*, which chronicled the 14-month journey of a woman who was detained and tortured by a satanic cult that her mother joined."

Canadian psychiatrist Lawrence Pazder wrote about his patient (and future wife) Michelle Smith. Pazder used recovered memory therapy for over six hundred hours' worth of sessions with Smith to bring up her "repressed" memories. Smith "remembered" her abuse starting at the hand of her mother at around the age of five. Later, she recounted tales of sexual and satanic ritual abuse by the Church of Satan, and then it turned into an elite group of powerful men and women who had children kidnapped for sexual favors, pornography, ritualistic abuse and human sacrifice. Some of her claims included being caged with snakes and watching the intentional slaughter of kittens before her eyes.

The best-selling memoir went viral, and Pazder toured with Michelle to promote the book. The pair ended up on *Oprah* and many other talk shows. They gave talks about how to spot satanic ritual abuse and what to do if you suspect someone in your neighborhood is conducting satanic rituals. Padzer was a consultant on many satanic ritual cases, including the McMartin Preschool Trial. Pazder and Smith even traveled to the Vatican to meet the pope.

As the years went by, much of the "memoir" was discredited. None of the allegations in the book lined up with real-life dates and timelines, nor was any proof ever presented to corroborate Smith's claims. In the end, the book was debunked and is now considered a piece of fiction.

During the same period, anticult spokesperson Patricia Pulling came forward to speak against role-playing games like *Dungeons and Dragons*. She started BADD (Bothered About *Dungeons and Dragons*) after her son died by suicide after shooting himself. She claimed that *Dungeons and Dragon* had brought demonology, witchcraft and satanism into her home. This perpetuated her son's declining mental health and eventual death. Pulling went so far as to file a lawsuit against her son's high school principal for letting role-playing games into the school. She then filed another lawsuit against TSR, the publishers of *Dungeons and Dragons*.

Later, the advocate mother wrote a book called the *Devil's Web: Who Is Stalking Your Children for Satan*, in which she added that police should investigate anyone who has a copy of the Necronomicon, because they are satanists. She also declared that 8 percent of the population were practicing Satanists, and 4 percent of them were teenagers. None of these statistics were ever proven to be true. Pulling died in 1997 from lung cancer, and BADD disbanded and was never revived.

The largest case during that time was the McMartin Preschool Trial. It started with allegations in 1983 and resulted in hundreds of accusations of satanic sexual abuse at the hands of the daycare. The investigation lasted for four years, from 1983 to 1987, and the trial lasted for three years, from 1987 to 1990. After a thorough investigative process, the McMartin trial became the most expensive criminal case in American history and resulted in *zero* convictions. By 1990, *all* charges were dropped.

The allegations started when a preschool mom reported that her son had been sodomized by her ex-husband and a teacher at the daycare named Ray Buckley. The mother had no proof of this, except her child was having painful bowel movements. She also accused the school of forcing the kids to have sex with animals. Buckley was arrested and questioned but not charged due to a lack of evidence.

Hundreds of children were interviewed, and 360 children were flagged for having experienced sexual abuse. Of those 360, only 41 actually testified in the trial. Some of the claims included sexual abuse, flying witches, rides in air balloons to undisclosed sites, underground tunnels that led to ritual rooms and satanic orgies. Chuck Norris was considered part of this elite satanic church and was identified as an abuser.

The interview process with the children was highly discredited, because the interviewers basically fed information to the kids via "scenarios" instead of asking for a straightforward retelling of memories. The "confessions" were largely coerced, and the kids were given clues about what the investigators wanted to hear. Most of the kids liked the attention and realized if they told the interviewers what they wanted to hear, they would get more attention.

In the end, no evidence was found for any of the allegations, and all charges were dropped by 1990. The mother who initially started the accusations was later hospitalized and diagnosed with paranoid schizophrenia and died of complications of alcoholism in 1996.

With Satanic Panic in full force, it makes sense that West Memphis believed the devil had finally made it to the small Arkansas town. When the three second graders were killed and left on the bank of Robin Hood Hills, the police went with what they had seen on television and in movies rather than sticking to typical investigating.

In cases like this, the killer is usually someone in the neighborhood, someone the kids knew and hung out with every day, like a father figure, an uncle or a close relative. That reality may have been too much for the West Memphis to deal with when it was easier to blame it on strange teenagers down the street who were largely misunderstood and fit the profile of satanists. It would be easier to pin it on them than realize the killers were living next door in plain sight. Man has always been more dangerous than the devil.

The following is a timeline of events, starting with the day the kids disappeared to their murder and ending with the West Memphis Three getting out of prison. This timeline spans years. So, I've added only the most important highlights.

Timeline

May 5, 1993: The Day the Three Boys Go Missing

2:55 p.m.: School ends at Weaver Elementary.

3:01 p.m.: Michael Moore walks home and meets up with his sister Dawn.

3:08 p.m.: Stevie walks home with his mom and sister Amanda.

3:11 p.m.: Chris is supposed to be home.

3:18 p.m.: Michael changes into his Boy Scout uniform.

3:28 p.m.: Michael goes to Stevie's house to play.

3:33 p.m.: Stevie and Michael leave on their bikes.

3:44 p.m.: Chris goes to Stevie's house and watches *The Muppet Show* with Amanda.

3:51 p.m.: Michael and Stevie play in the southeast part of the neighborhood.

4:02 p.m.: Chris goes to look for Michael and Stevie.

4:07 p.m.: The three boys meet on South McCauley Street.

4:18 p.m.: The boys are seen playing in the backyard of Jamie Clark Ballard.

4:30 p.m.: The boys are seen on Barton Street with another boy from the neighborhood.

4:31 p.m.: Chris heads home and breaks in through a window.

4:32 p.m.: Narleen Hollingsworth almost hits Michael and Stevie with her car.

4:36 p.m.: Michael goes home and looks for Chris.

4:43 p.m.: Michael and Chris are seen on Wilson Street, playing.

4:48 p.m.: Stevie arrives home late. He was supposed to be home at 4:30 p.m.

4:55 p.m.: Michael goes over to Tray's house.

5:03 p.m.: Chris is seen skateboarding with his neighbor Lakeisha.

5:10 p.m.: Stevie is most likely at home.

5:14 p.m.: Michael is on Holiday Drive with the fourth boy he was playing with earlier.

5:20 p.m.: Chris is picked up by his father and goes home.

5:30 p.m.: Chris gets punished and is forced to clean the carport.

5:36 p.m.: Michael is seen playing near the woods.

5:43 p.m.: Michael and the fourth boy talk to Alan Bailey Jr.

5:50 p.m.: Michael goes to find Chris.

5:56 p.m.: Michael and Stevie find each other on Wilson.

6:00 p.m.: The boys are seen on Fourteenth Street, headed toward Goodwin Street.

6:02 p.m.: Chris and Bobby Posey walk to Carlos's house.

6:07 p.m.: Michael and Stevie play near the entrance of the woods.

6:11 p.m.: Chris goes to Carlos's and finds out everyone is on Goodwin Street.

6:17 p.m.: Chris goes toward Goodwin Street to find his friends.

6:20 p.m.: Dana Moore sees all three kids together.

6:22 p.m.: All three boys are in Devils Den.

6:30 p.m.: The boys cross the pipe bridge.

8:00 p.m.: John Mark Byers calls the police about his son's disappearance.

8:30 p.m.: Byers goes looking around the woods for the boys.

9:00 p.m.: Dana Moore and Pam Hobbs call the police to report that their boys are missing.

Between 9:30 p.m. and 10:00 p.m.: Narline Hollingsworth tells police she saw Damien Echols and another boy walking near the Blue Beacon, which is on the edge of Robin Hood Hills.

THE MURDER

MAY 6, 1993

From 1:00 a.m. to 5:00 a.m.: The medical examiner Dr. Frank Peretti, who did the autopsy on the boys, says the murder likely took place at this time.

MAY 6, 1993

6:00 a.m.: Chief Inspector Gary Gitchell announces the boys are missing, and there will be search efforts.

1:45 p.m.: Officers find a body in Robin Hood Hills. Three bodies in total are found.

4:00 p.m.: The coroner arrives on the scene and declares all three boys dead. They were found in a ditch 150 yards from Blue Beacon Truck Wash, covered with approximately two and a half feet of water.

The Autopsies

Trigger Warning: The original wording of the autopsy report is clinical, thorough and graphic. This is a summary of the autopsy report, but it's still a hard read. If you are sensitive to medical details, I suggest you skip this part of the book and move on to the rest of the timeline.

Christopher Michael Byers

According to the autopsy, Byers died of "multiple injuries," and "homicide" was the manner of death. The second grader had Carbamazepine in his system, which is a drug used for epilepsy, nerve pain and bipolar disorder. There was no blood or semen present in his mouth or anus. Byers's body was received in the nude, and his hands were bound to his feet in a hogtie style. The second grader's right wrist was tied to his right ankle with a black shoelace, and his left wrist was tied to his left ankle with a white shoelace. His head was blood-soiled, and his body was covered with dried mud, leaves and other debris.

Byers's right ear was scraped and bruised. There were abrasions on his right eyebrow, left eyelid, left ear, nose and upper and lower lips, and there were bite marks on both of his cheeks. The top-left of his scalp had a laceration that showed hemorrhaging under the soft tissue. The base of the skull had multiple fractures.

Byers's anal orifice was dilatated, and his penis, scrotum and testes were missing. Both his left and right buttocks had abrasions and contusions. His left and right legs had bruising, as did parts of his lower back. The second grader's wrists and ankles had yellowed bruising from the hogties.

For the full autopsy report, you can go to this link: http://callahan.mysite.com/wm3/autcb.html.

Michael Moore

According to the autopsy report, Moore died of "multiple injuries with drowning," and "homicide" was the manner of death. No drugs were present in his system. His head was blood-soiled, and his body had spots of dried mud and some debris. Moore's wrists were bound to his ankles in a hogtie style with black shoelaces.

Punctuated scrapes were present on his nose, and his left cheek and lips had swollen contusions. On the front-right side of his head, the second grader had an egg-shaped swollen bruise with smaller lacerations. There was another egg-shaped bruise behind his right ear and smaller scratches on his lower face and jaw area. There were multiple bite wounds on the tip of his tongue.

Moore had multiple skull fractures, and the right side of his brain was swollen from hemorrhaging. The right side of his neck, shoulder and chest had scratches and bruising. The left side of his neck and his left abdomen had scratches.

The second grader's penis had no injuries, but his anal orifice was dilated. Upon further review, there seemed to be no internal injury to the anus. Also, the scrotum and testes were intact with no injuries. Moore had an egg-shaped bruise on his left knee and purple bruising on his ankles and wrists from the hogties. His back and buttocks had some scrapes and abrasions.

There was evidence of drowning in Moore's body. His sinus cavity had about two milliliters of water in it. His throat and chest area had hemorrhaging, and his lungs were swollen and exuding a frothy kind of material.

For the full autopsy report, go to: http://callahan.mysite.com/wm3/autmm.html.

Stevie Branch

According to the autopsy report, Branch died of "multiple injuries with drowning," and "homicide" was the manner of death. There were no drugs found in his system. The body was covered in leaves, mud and other debris. His hair was blond and had blood in it. Branch's penis, scrotum and testes were in good condition and intact. Branch's body was received in the nude, and his hands were bound to his feet in a hogtie style. The second grader's right wrist was tied to his right ankle with a black shoelace, and his left wrist was tied to his left ankle with a white shoelace.

The second grader had scratches and abrasions on his right ear, over his right eye and down the right side of his cheek. His lips were bruised and swollen, along with his gums. He had a dome-shaped cut on his left eyebrow with scrapes and bruises that went down the side of his face.

The left side of Branch's scalp had a large, swollen abrasion with overlying scratches. The neck and the base of the skull had fractures, mostly radiating from the left-hand side of the skull. His chest and lower left leg had scratches.

The second grader's lungs were swollen and filled with a bloody, frothy liquid. His sinuses were filled with a bloody water-like liquid. His wrists and ankles were swollen and yellowed from the bindings. There was no sperm or any other kind of sexual fluid present in any orifice or on his body.

For the full autopsy, go to: http://callahan.mysite.com/wm3/autsb.html.

AFTER THE MURDER

MAY 7, 1993

Juvenile Officer Steve Jones and Lieutenant Sudbury question Damien Echols about the death of the three boys but take no notes.

MAY 8, 1993

Detective Bill Durham and Investigator Shane Griffith question Damien Echols and Jason Baldwin about the deaths of the three boys. Echols and Baldwin tell the officials they've never heard of the kids who are dead.

MAY 10, 1993

Lieutenant Sudbury and Detective Byrn Ridge interview Damien Echols without a lawyer. He is given a polygraph test. According to Byrn's notes, Durham "reported that Damien had been untruthful, and according to the polygraph, participated in the murders."

MAY 12, 1993

Police interview Pam Echols, the mother of Damien Echols. She says that Echols was at home the night of the murders, talking on the phone with two girls from school.

MAY 19, 1993

Vicki Hutchinson, a neighbor of Jessie Miskelly, said she traveled with Damien Echols and Miskelly to an esbat, or a gathering of witches, in Marion, Arkansas. She said Echols drove all three of them there. There were ten other witches dressed in black with their faces and arms painted black there. According to Hutchinson, everyone took off their clothes and started touching each other. The esbat turned into an orgy. After the orgy, Hutchinson asked to be taken home, and Echols drove her home.

MAY 27, 1993

Police interview Vicki Hutchinson. She says that both Echols and Miskelly participate in cult activities. Hutchinson's son Aaron tells the police he often played in Robin Hood Hills with the murdered boys. He said, at times, he had seen five boys in the woods singing songs to the devil and engaging in "what men and ladies do."

JUNE 2, 1993

Hutchinson takes a polygraph test, and the police say she is truthful.

JUNE 3, 1993

Police interview Jesse Misskelley under false pretenses. They tell him there is a $35,000 reward for information leading to the arrest of the three boys' killer. Miselley denies being part of the murders or any kind of satanic rituals. The police think he is lying, and after many hours of harsh questioning, Miskelley bends. He tells the police what they want to hear, only there are large holes in his story, like the murders taking place during the day when they actually happened in the evening. Police nudge Miskelley into curating a narrative that follows the details of the case and then tape his "confession."

Go to this site if you would like to read the original confession in its entirety: https://www.dpdlaw.com/jessie-misskelley-jr-confession/.

JUNE 3, 1993, 9:00 P.M.

Police go in front of a judge and get search warrants for Damien, Jason and Jesse's homes.

JUNE 3, 1993, 10:30 P.M.

Damien, Jason and Jesse are arrested and charged with three counts of capital murder.

JUNE 4, 1993

The authorities hold a press conference, stating they've arrested the killers of the three boys. They are more than confident they have the right culprits.

JUNE 7, 1993

The three defendants are given lawyers.

JUNE 9, 1993

Eight-year-old Aaron Hutchinson is interviewed by the police. He says he saw the three boys being killed.

AUGUST 4, 1993

Damien, Jason and Jesse attended a pretrial hearing. Damien and Jason are to be tried together, and Jesse is to be tried separately. Judge Burnett decides Jesse's confession tape can be heard at all of the trials, even though it was taped under coercive circumstances. Also, all three boys are to be tried as adults.

SEPTEMBER 1993

The prosecution interviews the defendants' families and other witnesses under oath.

NOVEMBER 10, 1993

Judge Burnett decides Jesse's trial will be the first held in January, and then Damien and Jason will be tried in February.

NOVEMBER 17, 1993

The police hire divers to search the lake behind Damien and Jason's trailer park. They find a nine-inch serrated blade behind Jason's trailer.

DECEMBER 30, 1993

The defense interviews the Hutchinsons' neighbors, who say that Aaron was playing in the trailer park the day of the murders. He was not anywhere near close to Robin Hood Hills and couldn't have witnessed the boys getting killed.

JANUARY 18, 1994

Jury selection begins for Jesse's trial.

JANUARY 26, 1994

John Mark Byers is interviewed about a knife that had blood from his stepson, Christopher, and his own blood on it.

FEBRUARY 5, 1994

Jesse Miskelly is convicted of one count of first-degree murder and two counts of second-degree murder. He is sentenced to forty years in prison and is sent to a facility in Pine Bluff, Arkansas.

FEBRUARY 17, 1994

Jesse is pressured to say that he will testify in Damien and Jason's trial. He makes a statement under oath saying that the other teenagers killed the three boys.

FEBRUARY 18,1994

Jesse changes his mind and decides he doesn't want to testify at the other two teenagers' trial.

FEBRUARY 19,1994

Jury selection begins for Damien and Jason's trial.

FEBRUARY 28, 1994

Opening arguments begin for Damien and Jason's trial.

MARCH 17, 1994

Jury deliberations begin for Damien and Jason's trial.

MARCH 18, 1994

The jury comes back with a verdict of guilty. Damien and Jason are each charged with three counts of capital murder.

MARCH 21, 1994

In sentencing hearings, Jason is sentenced to life in prison, while Damien gets the death penalty. His death is scheduled for May 5, 1994. Jason is sent to the Pinebluff facility, while Damien is sent to death row in Varneer, Arkansas.

MAY 1994

All three teenagers appeal their convictions.

FEBRUARY 19, 1996

The Arkansas Supreme Court upholds Jesse's conviction.

1996

The film *Paradise Lost: The Child Murders of Robin Hills Hood* premieres. The website wm3.org goes up, and a movement to free Damien, Jason and Jesse is born.

DECEMBER 23, 1996

The Arkansas Supreme Court upholds Damien and Jason's convictions.

JUNE 17, 1999

Judge Burnett denies a petition to give Damien a new trial.

DECEMBER 1999

Damien marries Lorri Davis in a Buddhist ceremony in prison.

MARCH 2000

Paradise Lost 2: Revelations premieres. The movie questions whether John Mark Byers is the actual killer.

FEBRUARY 2001

Damien's attorney files erom coram nobis to the Arkansas Supreme Court, stating that the teenager shouldn't have been tried due to his mental state in 1994.

APRIL 2001

The Arkansas Supreme Court rules in favor of Damien and sends back a petition to Judge Burnett for consideration.

2002

Devil's Knot: The True Story of the West Memphis Three, a book by Mara Levitt, comes out.

OCTOBER 2003

Vicki Hutchinson tells an *Arkansas Times* reporter in an interview that she lied about everything she told the police. She said the police told her if she didn't say that Damien, Jason and Jesse were doing satanic rituals, she could have her son taken away.

2007

DNA evidence is tested. No DNA from Damien, Jason or Jesse are found on anything from the crime scene. A hair found in the knot of one of the shoelaces used to tie up one of the victims is connected to Terry Hobbs.

JULY 2008

Evidence shows the jury foreman of Damien and Jason's trial discussed the case with an attorney before deliberations and nudged the jury for a conviction.

SEPTEMBER 10, 2008

Judge Burnett denies a request for a new trial, stating the DNA evidence was inconclusive.

NOVEMBER 4, 2010

Based on the DNA evidence, the Arkansas Supreme Court orders the court to either give the three a new trial or exonerate them.

AUGUST 19, 2011

Damien, Jason and Jesse are released from prison as part of an Alford Plea.

2012

The movie *West of Memphis* premieres.

CONCLUSION

This book reveals the often-hidden side of this remarkable state, showcasing its dark past and haunted present. From the infamous West Memphis Three case to the mysterious Gurdon Light, Arkansas is a place where the paranormal and the unexplained converge.

Through the pages of this book, we explore the legends and lore that have shaped Arkansas's eerie reputation, from the ghostly spirits of Civil War soldiers to the elusive Bigfoot of the Ozarks. We have also delved into the history and culture of Arkansas, discovering the hidden stories that lie beneath the surface.

Despite its eerie reputation, Arkansas is a state full of natural beauty and vibrant communities. From the rugged Ozark Mountains to the rolling hills of the Arkansas Delta, Arkansas is a land of contrasts and diversity. It is a place where history and legend blend together, creating a tapestry of tales and experiences that are both eerie and captivating.

As we close the final chapter, let us remember that there is always more to discover, more mysteries to unravel and more stories to tell. In this world of ours, there is always something strange and fascinating just waiting to be explored.

BIBLIOGRAPHY

Websites

Abandoned Arkansas. "The Fee House." September 27, 2019. https://abandonedar.com/the-fee-house/.

American Battlefield Trust. "Battle of Pea Ridge." 2023. https://www.battlefields.org/learn/articles/battle-pea-ridge.

———. "Prairie Grove." 2023. https://www.battlefields.org/learn/civil-war/battles/prairie-grove.

Arkansas. "Legendary Monsters." 2023. https://www.arkansas.com/articles/legendary-monsters.

Arkansas Road Stories. "Grotto Spring." http://arkansasroadstories.com/springs/grotsp.html.

Arnn, Grace. "Searching For Souls: Cemetery Efforts Honor Formerly Enslaved." *Northwest Arkansas Democrat Gazette*, January 20, 2022. https://www.nwaonline.com/news/2022/jan/20/searching-for-souls-cemetery-efforts-honor/.

Associated Press. "Arkansas Man Says Dover Lights a Hoax." Arkansas Democrat Gazette, August 22, 2009. https://www.arkansasonline.com/news/2009/aug/22/arkansas-man-says-dover-lights-hoax/.

Atlas Obscura. "The Gurdon Light." October 14, 2013. https://www.atlasobscura.com/places/gurdon-light.

Blue Spring Heritage Center. "The History of the Spring Known as Blue Springs." https://www.bluespringheritage.com/history_spring.html.

Boggy Creek Monster Site. 2011–22. http://www.foukemonster.net/.

Bradley, Laura. "Inside the Horrific (Contested) Abuse Story that Ignited the Satanic Panic." *Daily Beast*. March 12, 2023. https://www.thedailybeast.com/satan-wants-you-sxsw-doc-abuse-story-that-ignited-the-satanic-panic.

Carson, Carol Ann. "The Arkansas Ghost Story That Will Leave You Absolutely Baffled." Only in Your State. January 23, 2018. https://www.onlyinyourstate.com/arkansas/ar-ghost-story-2/.

———. "No Actors Here, the Fee House in Arkansas Is Truly Haunted." August 31, 2022. https://www.onlyinyourstate.com/arkansas/ar-fee-haunted-house/.

———. "The Underwater Ruins in Monte Ne are a Strange Sight in Arkansas." Only in Your State. September 18, 2019. https://www.onlyinyourstate.com/arkansas/monte-ne-underwater-ruins/.

Choate, Laura. "West Memphis Three." *Encyclopedia of Arkansas*. 2023. https://encyclopediaofarkansas.net/entries/west-memphis-three-3039/.

Cox, Dale. "The Arkansas Airship Mystery of 1897." Explore Southern History. 2011. https://exploresouthernhistory.com/arkansasairship.html.

———. "The Resting Place of the Dead." Explore Southern History. 2011. https://www.exploresouthernhistory.com/fayettevillecc.html.

Crossett Light Blog. "The Amazing Crosset Light Directions." 2015. http://crossettlight.blogspot.com/p/the-amazing-crossett-light-directions.html.

Encyclopaedia Britannica. "History of Arkansas." 2023. https://www.britannica.com/place/Arkansas-state/History.

———. "West Memphis Three." April 5, 2023. https://www.britannica.com/event/West-Memphis-Three#ref1238667.

Encyclopedia of Arkansas. "Battle of Prairie Grove." 2023. https://encyclopediaofarkansas.net/entries/battle-of-prairie-grove-513/.

———. "Crossett Light." 2023. https://encyclopediaofarkansas.net/entries/crossett-light-5900/.

———. "David Walker." 2023. https://encyclopediaofarkansas.net/entries/david-walker-3237/.

———. "Fayetteville Confederate Cemetery." 2023. https://encyclopediaofarkansas.net/entries/fayetteville-confederate-cemetery-8104/.

———. "Fouke Monster." 2023. https://encyclopediaofarkansas.net/entries/fouke-monster-2212/.

Eureka Parks. "Springs." https://www.eurekaparks.com/copy-of-recreation-4.

Eureka Springs History. "Healing Springs." https://www.eurekasprings.com/historical/springs.html.

The Expelled. http://www.theexpelled.com/.

Experience Fayetteville. "Haunted Fayetteville." 2023. https://www.experiencefayetteville.com/experience/haunted-fayetteville.

Facebook. "Deanna Velten." August 3, 2022. https://m.facebook.com/photo.php?fbid=10228767899249512&id=1448526554&set=a.4008569499815&source=48&refid=17.

From the Vault. "Arkansas Histories Mysteries—Ghost Hollow." October 30, 2015. http://arkansasstatearchives.blogspot.com/2015/10/arkansas-historys-mysteries-ghost-hollow.html.

———. "Arkansas Histories Mysteries—The Mystery of the Mena Poltergeist." April 1, 2016. http://arkansasstatearchives.blogspot.com/2016/04/arkansas-historys-mysteries-mystery-of.html.

Galiano, Amanda. "The Ghosts of Arkansas: Gurdon Light. Trip Savvy." January 2, 2019. https://www.tripsavvy.com/gurdon-light-2211874.

Hathorn, Tiffany. "Arkansas Folklore: Monster Edition." Only in Arkansas. June 20, 2016. https://onlyinark.com/culture/arkansas-folklore-monster-edition/.

Hill, Martin David. "The Place." JivePuppi. 2008. https://www.jivepuppi.com/jivepuppi_the_place.html.

Historical Marker Database. "Sweet Spring." 2006–23. https://www.hmdb.org/m.asp?m=80115.

Johnson, Lauren. "Go Ghosting Hunting in This Downtown Little Rock House Until It Turns into a Bed and Breakfast." TV11. October 3, 2019. https://www.thv11.com/article/entertainment/go-ghost-hunting-in-this-downtown-little-rock-house/91-c487a22d-5f4a-4307-952f-e4bec19bcf1e.

Johnson, Melanie. "An Unexpected Grotto Is Hiding Underground in this Cavern in Arkansas." Only in Your State. January 5, 2023. https://www.onlyinyourstate.com/arkansas/underground-grotto-ar/.

Lake Ouachita. "Three Sisters Springs Lake Ouachita." 2023. https://lakeouachita.org/3-sisters-springs-lake-ouachita/.

Legends of America. "Arkansas Civil War Battles." 2023. https://www.legendsofamerica.com/arkansas-civil-war-battles/.

Linder, Douglas O., professor. "West Memphis 3 Trials—A Chronology." Famous Trials. 1995–2023. https://famous-trials.com/westmemphis/2236-chronology.

McLarty Daniel Buick GMC. "Monsters of Arkansas." 2023. https://www.bentonvillebuickgmc.com/blog/monsters-of-arkansas-mclarty-daniel-551950.

Mr. Spooky. "The Ghost of Monte Ne: Dear Darla." Spooky NWA. October 10, 2018. https://spookynwa.com/the-ghost-of-monte-ne-dear-darla/.

New Age Magazine. https://play.google.com/books/reader?id=JL9NAAAAMAAJ&pg=GBS.RA1-PA206&hl=en.

Newman, Hugh. "Top Ten Giant Discoveries in North America." Ancient Origins. February 12, 2022. https://www.ancient-origins.net/unexplained-phenomena/giants-north-america-005196.

Ramano, Aja. "Why Satanic Panic Never Really Ended." Vox. March 31, 2021. https://www.vox.com/culture/22358153/satanic-panic-ritual-abuse-history-conspiracy-theories-explained.

Rivera, Geraldo. "Devil Worship: Exposing Satan's Underground." IMDB. October 22, 1988. https://www.imdb.com/title/tt1136645/.

Sain, Johnny Carol. "Shedding Illumination on the Dover Lights." About the River Valley, October 1, 2011. https://aboutrvmag.com/2011/10/01/shedding-illumination-on-the-dover-lights/.

Shakedown. "West Memphis 3." https://shakedowntitle.com/cases/west-memphis-3/.

Shiloh Museum of Ozark History. "Healing Waters Online Exhibit." 2023. https://shilohmuseum.org/project/healing-waters/.

Siloam Springs Museum. "The Siloam Spring in Siloam Springs." https://www.siloamspringsmuseum.com/found-in-the-archives/the-siloam-spring-in-siloam-springs.

Weiser-Alexander, Kathy. "Hot Springs, Arkansas." Legends of America. March 2020. https://www.legendsofamerica.com/hot-springs-arkansas/.

Wikipedia. "Arkansas in the American Civil War." https://en.wikipedia.org/wiki/Arkansas_in_the_American_Civil_War.
———. "Battle of Pea Ridge." https://en.wikipedia.org/wiki/Battle_of_Pea_Ridge.
———. "Fayetteville Confederate Cemetery." https://en.wikipedia.org/wiki/Fayetteville_Confederate_Cemetery.
———. "Fouke Monster." https://en.wikipedia.org/wiki/Fouke_Monster.
———. "History of Arkansas." https://en.wikipedia.org/wiki/History_of_Arkansas.
———. "Legend of Boggy Creek." https://en.wikipedia.org/wiki/The_Legend_of_Boggy_Creek.
———. "McMartin Preschool Trial." https://en.wikipedia.org/wiki/McMartin_preschool_trial.
———. "Michele Remembers." https://en.wikipedia.org/wiki/Michelle_Remembers.
———. "Monte Ne." https://en.wikipedia.org/wiki/Monte_Ne.
———. "Patricia Pulling." https://en.wikipedia.org/wiki/Patricia_Pulling.
———. "Satanic Panic." https://en.wikipedia.org/wiki/Satanic_panic.
———. "West Memphis Three." https://en.wikipedia.org/wiki/West_Memphis_Three.
———. "William Hope Harvey." https://en.wikipedia.org/wiki/William_Hope_Harvey.

BOOKS

Lord, Allyn. *Historic Monte Ne*. Rogers, AK: Rogers Historical Museum, 2006.
Young, Richard, and Judy Dockrey Young. *The Burning Bride: Ozark Ghost Stories*. Atlanta, GA: August House Publishers, 1992.

VIDEOS

Berg, Amy, dir. *West of Memphis*. Culver City, CA: Sony Pictures, 2012.
Berlinger, Joe, and Bruce Sinofsky, dirs. *Paradise Lost*. New York: HBO, 1996.
———. *Paradise Lost 2: Revelations*. New York: HBO, 2000.
———. *Paradise Lost 3: Purgatory*. New York: HBO, 2011.
Crime Retracer. "West Memphis 3—Map of Events." 2018. https://youtu.be/DMrdqVsRcsg.
Old State House Museum. "UFO Sightings in 1897 Arkansas." 2016. https://youtu.be/FFkhH7t7e0w.

About Heather Woodward

HEATHER WOODWARD, award-winning clairvoyant psychic, channeler and medium, has conducted over thirty thousand readings and aided numerous clients with their most pressing issues. The psychic is also certified as a life coach, a crystal healing practitioner and a Rose Priestess working with the Magdalene Rose lineage. She is known for consistently working with her Pleiadean guides, the Blue Rays and the Ascended Masters in the Sisterhood of the Rose. For more information on her readings, interested individuals can visit www.heatherashera.com or listen to her podcast at www.nvusalien.com.

About Kelli Welsh

Kelli Welsh is an Ozarks native with nearly a decade of experience as an agnostic witch and healer. As a trauma survivor, she uses traditional and intuited practices to aid in trauma processing and deepen our reverence for the natural wilds.